£8-50

D0786769

Asian Patients in Hospital and at Home

King Edward's Hospital Fund for London

Patron Her Majesty The Queen

Governors HRH Princess Alexandra, The Hon Mrs Angus Ogilvy GCVO
Sir Andrew H Carnwath KCVO DL
Lord Cottesloe GBE TD

Treasurer R J Dent

Chairman of the Management Committee Lord Hayter KCVO CBE

Secretary G A Phalp CBE TD

King Edward's Hospital Fund for London is an independent foundation, established in 1897 and incorporated by Act of Parliament 1907, and is a registered charity. It seeks to encourage good practice and innovation in the management of health care by research, experiment and education, and by direct grants.

Appeals for these purposes continue to increase.

The Treasurer would welcome any new sources of money, in the form of donations, deeds of convenant or legacies, which would enable the Fund to augment its activities.

Requests for the annual report, which includes a financial statement and lists of all grants, and other information, should be addressed to the Secretary, King Edward's Hospital Fund for London, 14 Palace Court, London W2 4HT.

Asian Patients
in Hospital
and at Home

By Alix Henley

King Edward's Hospital Fund for London

© King Edward's Hospital Fund for London 1979

Produced by Pitman Medical Publishing Co Ltd, Tunbridge Wells, Kent

Printed and bound in England by The Pitman Press, Bath

British Library Cataloguing in Publication Data
Henley, Alix
   Asian patients in hospital and at home.
   1. South Asians in Great Britain 2. Minorities—
   Medical care—Great Britain.
   I. Title II. King Edward's Hospital Fund
   for London.
   301.45'19'14041   DA125.S57

ISBN (

Distributed for the King's Fund by
Pitman Medical Publishing Co Ltd

King's Fund Publishing Office
126 Albert Street, London NW1 7NF

Note on the author

Alix Henley works at the Industrial Unit of the Pathway Further Education Centre, Southall, Middlesex, teaching English as a second language to workers in industry. She is a graduate of the University of London, where she read English, and has spent three years teaching English in Thailand. She is presently working on a special project, supported by King Edward's Hospital Fund for London and the Department of Health and Social Security, to prepare training materials for nurses and other health care professionals who work with Asian patients from the Indian subcontinent and East Africa.

Acknowledgments

Most of all, I should like to thank Liz Laird, who is responsible for much of the material, and who started me off writing the book. It would be impossible to list all the people who have spared so much of their time to answer my questions. Among them are David Bonamy, Evelyn Davies, Tom Jupp, Ce Roberts and everyone else at the Pathway Further Education Centre; Marlene Hinshelwood, Vivienne Coombe and Celia Pyke-Lees, Commission for Racial Equality; Taro Brah, National Association for Asian Youth; Geeta Amin, Wandsworth Council for Community Relations; Subash Patel, Brent Indian Association; Fatma Dharamsi, Harlesden Community Project; Shameem Khan, Slough Industrial Language Training Centre; Ann Mathias, Manchester Industrial Language Training Centre; Ted Gang, Department of Health and Social Security; and Elizabeth Anionwu, Lily Khan, Ann Loynes, Nichola Ruck and Verity Saifullah Khan.

I should also like to thank Jenny, Sue, Richard and my family, for their boundless patience and support.

The contents of the book are my responsibility and comments or questions from readers should be addressed to me at Pathway Further Education Centre, Recreation Road, Southall, Middlesex UB2 5PF.

AH
1979

Contents

Figures

Maps

Introduction

Hospital and community health services in nearly every large town in Britain are now caring for Asian patients from India, Pakistan, Bangladesh and East Africa. Most of them have grown up in societies and cultures very different from those of most of the nurses and doctors who care for them in Britain. There is often also a language barrier which adds to the problems of understanding.

British hospitals and health services have developed to fit the needs of British patients. Like many other institutions, once founded, they tend to develop a life and inflexible structure of their own. There are powerful moves towards making hospitals and other services less inflexible and more 'patient-centred'—more responsive to the needs and wishes of the patients—but the changes made are largely for the benefit of the majority population. Members of the immigrant groups may benefit from the increased flexibility, but few provisions have been made with their needs specifically in mind.

One reason for this is that many British institutions expect people to fit in with them, however alien and difficult this may in fact be for people from other cultures. Another reason is that, both at an institutional and at an individual level, there is a real lack of reliable information about the problems and the needs of Asian communities in Britain, as well as a failure to understand the *nature* of cultural differences and the degree of adaptation that can or cannot reasonably be expected.

At an individual level many health workers find it difficult to understand and to cater for the particular needs and expectations of their Asian patients. Again, this is frequently because they have no reliable information to work from and so cannot know what their patients need. In addition, because they are working across barriers of culture and language they may themselves find their work more difficult and less satisfying. They may be working under increased pressure.

This book aims to fill some of the information gaps.

British health workers share all kinds of values and attitudes with their British patients. As a result, they are able to understand and cater for the patients' needs, and to understand them individually.

With Asian patients, there are very many general questions to which British health workers do not have the answers. What do Hindus believe? How are Moslem names different from British names? What worries Indian patients about British hospitals? Unless health workers know the answers to general questions like these, it is difficult for them to begin to cater for the needs of their Asian patients in the same individual way as they do for their British patients.

On the other hand, it is as misleading to talk about 'Asian' culture as it is to talk about 'European' culture. And it is dangerous to make generalisations about people's likely attitudes and reactions. Compare, for example, the value and credibility that we might give to a book for health workers in India that claimed to deal with the 'culture of European patients'. The generalisations that would be made in such a book might have some truth, but we would find it very difficult to accept them all as applicable to ourselves. Patterns of cultural and social behaviour are often easy to see from the outside, but may not, to people who know the whole picture from the inside, seem at all accurate. Furthermore, you cannot treat individuals on the basis of generalisations about their culture, but you have to know the culture in order to understand the individual brought up within it.

Every Asian immigrant has already made major adaptations in life-style and outlook. As time passes, people are continually adapting, often to a degree which surprises themselves but which may be unappreciated by others. Much of this book will, therefore, apply only to people during their early years in Britain, or to those who lead sheltered lives in this country. Most adult immigrants find that it is the practical adjustment to a new country which is the easiest to make. They are far less likely ever to change the most important values and ways of the society in which they grew up.

1 Who are they?
Where do they come from?

The term 'Asian' is used in this book to cover the major groups of Asians in Britain from the Indian subcontinent (India, Pakistan, and Bangladesh) and from East Africa.

The book does not refer to people who have come from all over Asia to Britain as qualified professionals, nor primarily to Asians who were born or have grown up in this country, but to the people who have the greatest difficulty in adapting to life in Britain: people who have emigrated as adults from villages in the Indian subcontinent or have come as a result of political developments in East Africa.

Most people from the Indian subcontinent come from only a few relatively prosperous rural areas. Within those areas, certain villages have a tradition of emigration. In general, people have come from one occupational group—small owner-farmers. The areas vary a good deal in prosperity, in educational and health facilities, and in the amount of contact with urban areas and the world outside. Religious differences and historical factors also affect the social values and attitudes in the different groups.

Most Asians from East Africa have come from the towns and cities; they formed a largely commercial middle class, but with tremendous variations in wealth and in their ways of life. Though

Figure 1 MAIN ASIAN COMMUNITIES IN BRITAIN (see Maps 1 and 2)

People from	are called	their religion	their first language	they may speak some	they first settled in
INDIA *Punjab*	Punjabis	Sikhism or Hinduism	Punjabi*	Hindi	Chatham, Gravesend and Rochester Leeds Maidenhead Smethwick Southampton Warwick and Leamington Spa West London West Midlands Coventry Leeds
Gujarat Central and Southern Regions	Gujaratis	mainly Hinduism, some Islam	Gujarati*.	Hindi	*Gujarati Hindus* Birmingham Leicester North London Preston South-east England Wellingborough West Bromwich West Midlands
Northern Region (Kutch)	Kutchis or Gujaratis	mainly Hinduism, some Islam	Kutchi or Gujarati*	Gujarati* Hindi	*Gujarati Moslems* Bolton Leicester Preston Tameside Wandsworth (London)
PAKISTAN *Punjab*	Punjabis	Islam	Punjabi	Urdu*	Bedford Glasgow High Wycombe Humberside Lancashire Maidenhead Sheffield Slough West Midlands West Yorkshire
Mirpur (Azad Kashmir)	Mirpuris	Islam	Mirpuri (Punjabi dialect)	Punjabi Urdu*	
North West Frontier Province	Pathans	Islam	Pashto	Urdu* Punjabi	

6

| **BANGLADESH** (mainly from Sylhet district) | Bengalis | Islam | Bengali* | Bolton Bradford Dundee East and North-east London Keithley Luton Oldham Scunthorpe Sheffield Tameside |
| **EAST AFRICA** Kenya Malawi Tanzania Uganda Zambia | Hinduism, Islam or Sikhism depending on family origin | either Gujarati or Punjabi depending on family origin | Hindi* English* Swahili | Birmingham Croydon Leicester Loughborough North and South London South-east England |

* Language spoken at school.

Notes: There are also small groups from

1 the South Indian coastal state of Kerala, who are mostly Hindus and speak Malayalam, a Southern Indian language completely unrelated to the Northern Indian language

2 the coastal area around Bombay, who are mostly Moslem and may speak Marati, Gujarati or Kutchi

3 Delhi and surrounding areas, whose first language is Hindi

4 Lahore and other cities in Pakistan, whose first language is Urdu and who may also speak a local language

5 East Africa, whose families originated in Goa and who are Roman Catholics and whose first language is usually English.

Most Indian restaurants are owned and staffed by people from Bangladesh.

See also Figure 11 (page 163), Relationships between Asian languages, and Figure 12 (page 165), Written forms of Asian languages.

7

Map 1   MAIN EMIGRATION AREAS IN THE INDIAN SUBCONTINENT

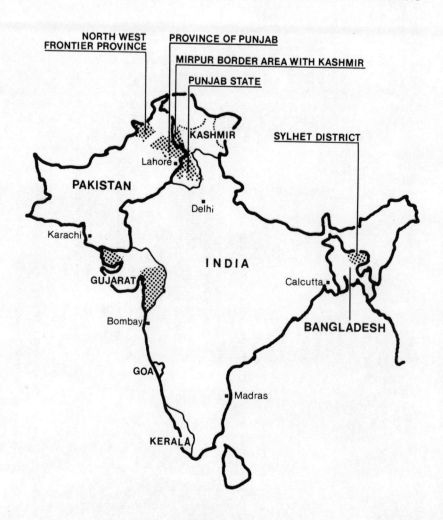

Map 2   MAIN EMIGRATION AREAS IN EAST AFRICA

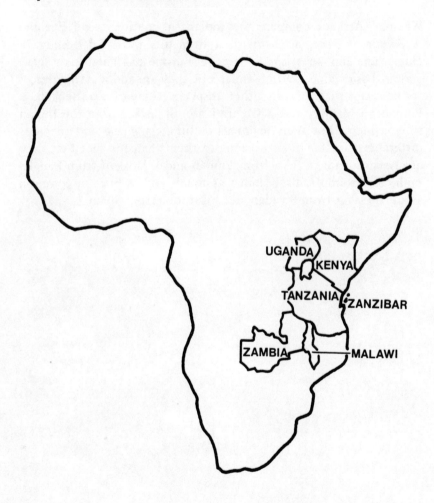

we refer to all these people as 'Asians', it is important to remember that this is not how they see themselves. To them, the differences between them are glaringly obvious, and far more important than the similarities.

We may perhaps compare the Indian subcontinent and Europe. A Swede, a Scot, a Spaniard, a Frenchman, an Englishman, a Hungarian and an Irishman are all Europeans. They may share certain basic values and attitudes but they are and feel themselves to be very different in other respects. Similarly, a Bengali, a Punjabi, a Mirpuri and a Gujarati are all Asians from the Indian subcontinent, but their regional, cultural, language and religious differences are far more obvious to them than the fact that they are Asians. Thus, a Sikh from Punjab and a Moslem from Bangladesh, for example, have about as much and as little in common as a Protestant from Sweden and a Catholic from Spain.

2 Asian families at home

The extended family

The extended family is the centre of all Asian cultures. Its values remain central to most Asians in Britain. It is traditionally the most important thing in each person's life, and has the strongest influence on his behaviour and outlook.

In the Indian subcontinent, each family usually consists of three generations. The head of the family and his wife, their sons, their sons' wives and children live together in one household (see Figure 2). As each generation grows up, the sons marry and bring their wives into the extended family household; the daughters leave home to marry and to live in their husbands' extended families.

Figure 2   AN EXTENDED FAMILY HOUSEHOLD

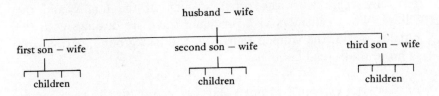

Note: This is the basic household; it may also include unmarried daughters, widows, orphaned children and other relatives.

When the head of the family dies, his sons may decide to remain together and to maintain one farm and one household. They may, alternatively, choose to divide their land and form separate households. Whether or not the household splits, the bonds and mutual obligations between the family members remain strong. There are also strong bonds with other, more distant, relatives. This whole group, what we would define as the 'extended family', is to most Asians merely the normal 'family'.

Men and women

The roles of men and women are clearly separate, with defined areas of responsibility and different duties. The men are responsible for working on the family farm, or in the business, and for bringing in the money. They are responsible for all contact with the world outside the family or the village, and with all public authorities. They are the public spokesmen for the family.

Women are responsible for the day-to-day care of the family and household. They look after children and the old. On the farm, they cook, clean, spin, weave, make clothes, milk the cows and so on. All the women of the house work together under the authority of the wife of the head of the family. Anyone who is ill, or pregnant, or has a young child, can rest while the other women take over her chores. Women are responsible for the religious and moral upbringing of the children and often for performing many of the family's religious obligations. Women generally relax with the other women of the family and the village. When outsiders visit, or when there are dealings with the outside world, the women remain in the background, particularly in more traditional families.

In East Africa, most women did not work at all, even in the home, and their household chores were generally done by African servants. Some East African Asian women had careers, particularly in medicine and teaching. Most of them, however, led a leisurely life.

Authority

Decisions are made communally, but the head of the household has the ultimate say. All the members fit into a hierarchy in which older people have authority over younger people, and (depending on their age) men have authority over women. For example, the wife of a younger brother should respect and obey the wife of an older brother. Every member has a defined status: this influences his behaviour towards the other members and the attention they give to his views when decisions are being made.

Money

All income and property belong to the whole family. Even where a family maintains more than one household, members still feel strong obligations to support each other financially. Money is lent or given to whoever needs it, whenever he needs it. Family members who are old or cannot support themselves are supported by the other members. Adult members feel responsible, for example, for the children of their brothers, sisters or cousins, and will look after them if the need arises.

Moral obligation, responsibility and dependency

In this strong system of mutual responsibility and obligation, each member considers himself a part of his family rather than an independent individual. His priorities are the happiness and reputation of his family and all its members, and these take precedence over his own needs and ambitions. He should act with an unselfish regard for the good of the whole family. Any action of his affects all the members, and must be considered in that light. He is not free to make important decisions by himself and must always consult his family. Every adult in the family is involved in any important decision. This extends even to the kind of action that we might consider entirely a matter of personal choice, and is particularly important in the case of marriage.

The basic needs of every individual, all through his life, are fulfilled within his extended family. No one need ever feel isolated, and no one ever loses his dependency on the other members of his family, nor they on him.

Marriage

An Asian girl who marries is entering into a very different partnership from that of a western bride. A western marriage is a close, intensely personal, exclusive union between a man and woman who will depend chiefly on each other for all their emotional, physical and economic needs.

An Asian wife is in many ways marrying the whole family. It is vital that she should be the kind of person who will fit into a large close-knit household and be happy there for the rest of her life. She will spend most of her time with the other women and she will bring up her children and grow old with them. Her affections, loyalty and obligations to the other members of the family are as important as those to her spouse.

The marital relationship, though important, is not the only relationship to be considered. The husband's whole family is taking in a new and permanent member, and the choice of that new member must, therefore, be a family decision. On the girl's side, her father is committing her for the rest of her life to the care and protection of a new family, upon which she will depend for all her emotional, physical and financial needs. After the marriage the two families will be firmly linked and will have certain mutual responsibilities.

Most Asians feel that such an important decision as marriage is not a matter which a young and inexperienced boy or girl should have to make. The young are too easily swayed by changeable emotions and irrational feelings. On the other hand, if the two families choose wisely they will unite a young couple who will develop a close and loving relationship as they get to know each other. Their partnership will enrich the family.

This is the traditional pattern; but it is changing, both in the subcontinent and in Britain. Couples are marrying at a later age, by which time they are considered more capable of making wise decisions about marriage themselves, and are given an increasing amount of choice. Both sides usually have an opportunity to cry off before a commitment is made. Even so, most Asian parents of all groups still see arranged marriages as the only sensible way. Moslem families have generally remained more conservative about arranged marriages than the other groups.

Broken marriages and divorce

Arranged marriages do not always succeed: they seem, however, to be at least as successful as western 'love matches' which are looked upon with fear and suspicion by most Asian parents. A broken marriage is always sad. But it has more repercussions in an extended family than in a western-style family. The extended family may be seen as the equivalent of the welfare state for all its members. It is the sole source of support for the young, the old and the infirm. A broken marriage threatens every member of the family and may even threaten his or her support. The break may be regarded as the fault of the wife, since it is traditionally her duty to adapt and fit in.

In Hindu and Sikh communities, marriage is regarded as an indissoluble sacrament. Divorce is permitted by law but is rare. Under Islamic law, marriage is a contract, not a sacrament, and divorce is more frequent. Islamic law makes provision for the support of a divorced wife: at marriage the bridegroom's family promises a sum of money to the bride which will be given to her if the marriage should break up.*

In all groups, the family and the community have a duty to do all they can to save the marriage. In Britain, because Asian communities are more fragmented, community support and concern are often lacking. Women feeling the stigma of divorce, and families with marital problems, may well have nowhere to turn for support and advice.

Death of the husband

In Hindu and Sikh cultures, women must withdraw from community life when their husbands die. Hindu widows should shave their heads, wear white clothes, perform their religious duties more strictly, including the observance of dietary taboos, and should remain secluded at home. Remarriage is out of the question. For Moslem women, widowhood carries no such social burdens. Like Hindu and Sikh widows, a Moslem widow must remain strictly secluded for three or four months, but she may then resume her place in the community, and is encouraged to remarry.

Children

In the subcontinent, most children grow up looked after by all the women and by elder cousins, brothers and sisters. A baby is carried by its mother most of the time and is suckled whenever it

* See also Chapter 4, Religion, pages 31–52.

cries. It is believed that to allow a child to cry may weaken it. The women and children spend most of the day together out in the courtyard. There is plenty of fresh air and space for the children. They do not need manufactured toys or 'guided play'. There may be little emphasis on 'potty training'. There is always someone around when a child wants a cuddle. When the younger women are busy, the older women, and often the older men, will watch over the children.

Children are always included in any outing or festivity. They do not have a special schedule or routine. They sleep with their parents and go to bed when they do. It is considered cruel to make a young child sleep apart from its mother.

Until a child is about five, everything is done for him: he is washed, dressed, fed, cuddled and carried and is not expected to cope by himself. After the age of five, he will be expected to begin to look after himself and to keep an eye on any younger children. Discipline becomes increasingly strong and is seen as a positive thing. Most Asian parents believe that loving a child means disciplining him. They may use corporal punishment, and parental rule is generally authoritarian. Children know exactly what they can and cannot do. This contrasts very much with the emphasis on self-discipline in many British families.

The problems associated with adolescence in western society do not exist in traditional Asian cultures. Young people are expected to move directly from childhood to adulthood.

Sons and daughters

In many societies the birth of a son is regarded as a greater blessing than that of a daughter. This is still true in Britain in many areas. Sons are more important in traditional farming societies in which ownership of land is carried through the male line. A family without sons loses its land and its possessions, and disappears. Boys are potential workers for the family; they will bring wives into the family, father new family members and support the older members when they can no longer support themselves. Among Hindus, a son is required to perform the death rites for his parents. To be without a son to do this is a terrible stroke of fate.

Daughters, though much loved, will leave the family when they marry. A girl cannot contribute to the family income, and in some communities a large dowry must be found if she is to make a good marriage. A family with several daughters can be financially ruined. Women who have given birth to several daughters, but no sons, may become so depressed that they reject another female child.

A girl is brought up to be respectful and obedient to her elders and to all men. On her marriage she will have to fit into a new household where she will be the lowest in the pecking order. She must be amenable and adaptable. Nobody will want to marry a girl with a reputation for being headstrong. She must be completely chaste. Even going out alone or to a youth club might harm her reputation. She may only go out with other girls or with an elder brother. The reputation of a family lies particularly with its daughters, and the bad reputation of one daughter can affect the chances of marriage of all the others. Girls may be materially spoilt, but their freedom is restricted, and any disobedience or lack of modesty is punished. Daughters must help their mothers with the household chores and must take care of the younger siblings.

Sons have a good deal more freedom to go out and make friends outside, though a strict code of moral behaviour is expected. They are expected to show obedience and respect, but they are also trained to have authority and to become responsible for dealings with the world outside the family.

Brothers and sisters have a strong bond. There are important ceremonies in which brothers promise to care for their sisters and to protect them all their lives. One of a brother's greatest duties is to fulfil this promise.

Attitudes towards daughters are beginning to change in the Indian subcontinent now that women can inherit a share of the family land under the law, and can go out to work and contribute to the family. The financial burden of several daughters is, therefore, beginning to lessen. However, long-established social attitudes towards the birth of a daughter are likely to take some time to disappear.

In Britain, attitudes are changing more rapidly. Girls here have more or less equal opportunities and can go out to work. But the rest of the family in the subcontinent will still be judging things along strictly traditional lines. To them a son means continuity and sure support.

3 Asian families in Britain

When a son and his wife and children emigrate they remain part of the extended family, and the family home remains, in a very real sense, their home and the centre of their life. They have gone out as a part of the family, usually as the result of a family decision, and they will try to give priority to the needs of the family household. They will send money for improvements on the farm. They will consult and respect the judgment of the head of the family though he may be in a small village over 4000 miles away. This is true even of communities like the Gujaratis and Sikhs who are scattered all over the world and who have had a tradition of travel and migration for several hundred years.

Asian parents in Britain will often be concerned that their children should grow up in the way that the rest of the family back in the subcontinent would approve. The verdict of the head of the family is likely to remain most important to Asian parents in this country.

Adaptation

An immigrant family arriving in this country takes on the problems and pressures of everyone else in the area where it settles. In addition, the family has to cope with the problems of separation, loneliness, language, and a complete change of climate and routine.

The effect of immigration on the structure of the family itself will vary from family to family. There is no doubt, however, that the roles of individuals within the family alter a great deal. Each person has to make his or her own adaptation. Although from the outside an Asian family may appear unified, the pressures and different experiences of each member are often pulling it apart. The strength and support of the family protects all its members, but when the family is split, or where all members are under great stress, it may lose its supportiveness.

The differences between life in the home village and in Britain are likely to cause most stress to the husband and wife of the immigrant family.

The husband

He may not, in terms of the extended family, be the real head.

Because of language problems and lack of technical skills, he may be in a low-status, low-paid job.

He is usually not working with the other men of his family, or is not his own boss.

He is responsible for making the move a success.

He is under financial pressure: he may be sending money home while taking on the heavy new financial commitments of a householder in Britain.

Because of the changes and compromises he makes in Britain, and because he is aware of racialism outside his house, he is likely to be the more anxious to preserve continuity and stability within it.

He is not in authority in the same way. Much of his traditional role has been taken over by the state or local authorities, but he has the complicated new responsibilities of living in an urbanised, bureaucratic society.

He may feel his children are growing away from him and that his family in Britain is growing away from his extended family in Asia.

His heart and mind may still be with the extended family and the farm or village, and these may be unimportant to his children.

The wife

She shares many of her husband's problems but may have additional stresses because of her different role in Britain.

She may have rejoined her husband after a separation of many years. He may have been living alone here, saving hard to bring his family over and he may have changed a great deal.

She may feel she is not giving her family the standard of care that is her duty: she may find it difficult to cope with the change in housing, climate, shopping and so on.

She may be going out to work, combining the role of a working wife with that of a woman in an extended family. She will generally not do any less in the home and will work hard to maintain her domestic standards. Other members of her family, particularly the husbands and parents-in-law, may not understand the problems of a working wife and may still expect the same kind of service from her around the house. She may also be influenced by her position as a wage earner and by the greater freedom of British women, and may resent the traditional role expected of her.

She may remain isolated at home and rarely go out. She may have no opportunity to find out about the society in which she now lives and of which her family is now part.

She may not have the female companionship she was used to at home. She may be coping with a house and family on her own for the first time in her life. Her husband may have more outlets outside and may not understand his wife's loneliness. She is likely to be particularly dependent on him in Britain because she is used to having him deal with everything outside the home. Outside affairs are generally both more onerous and more complicated in an urban, industrial society.

Her main satisfaction is generally as a mother, the centre of the home. But her children spend most of the day away from home and are increasingly pulled away from her. She loses her main source of happiness and satisfaction. While her family is adapting, she may not be.

Some women in Britain have relatives living nearby and this usually provides a good deal of support. Some communities, particularly those which have been settled for some time, are also more cohesive than others. In general, however, self-help groups and other systems of support have not yet developed. Many Asian women still see the family as the only possible source of support and help, and do not know what to do when it is not there. They do not feel that they can turn to non-family members, even of their own community. At home, people rarely, if ever, go outside their own family or village for help.

The children

Instead of being able to play all day in a large sunny courtyard, Asian children in Britain spend most of their days indoors until they reach school age.

Their adaptation to life in Britain brings problems of a different kind. Most adapt to living in two cultures, and choose to belong to one or the other, depending on whom they are with. This works as long as neither their families nor the host society puts pressure on them to choose one way and reject the other. For some children, however, the conflicting demands of two cultures become destructive.

At home, they are taught the value of obedience, and learning by watching. They learn to be concerned always for the family and for their younger brothers and sisters. Communalism, cooperation, dependence and sharing are valued: competition and individual ambition are not.

At school, things are very different. Children are taught to question rules and to work out their own code of behaviour. They learn by questioning and discussing. People in authority are not automatically given respect. Children are expected to compete with their peers and to work for individual success. They are expected to show initiative, to make decisions, to learn from their mistakes and to develop their own potential. They are very much influenced by their peers, and their ambitions run to parties, pop music, boyfriends and girlfriends, experiment and freedom. Many Asian parents are horrified to hear that their teenage daughter mixes freely with boys at school, and their daughter may say that she does not. At the same time, girls may invent imaginary boyfriends to impress their friends at school. Asian parents generally have very high expectations of their children at school, though they may not know much about what happens there or about the educational system.

Asian children growing up here often pick up some of the stereotype attitudes of their English peers towards India, Pakistan and Bangladesh. They may believe that they are povery-stricken places full of primitive, lazy peasants to whom Britain and the rest of the western world keep sending aid. They may, in addition, have picked up racist attitudes and be prejudiced against people of their own colour. They may look down upon their own parents as uneducated and inferior. They may reject their own culture and be ashamed of it and of their families. They may refuse to speak their mother tongue. In some cases young Asians may refuse to go home with their parents to visit the rest of the family. Their attempts to identify totally with British culture and society are, however, almost bound to fail, particularly since racism and racial discrimination are very real features of British society.

As they grow up, they must contend with other conflicting attitudes. According to British culture, the money you earn is yours to do with what you want. Your job is an important part of your life in which you can develop your own ambitions and abilities. You live your life so as to develop your individuality and potential. You experiment with sexual relationships of varying intensity and seriousness. And you marry because you are in love.

Asian views of western marriage

Many Asian parents in Britain look upon western 'love marriages' and sexual morality with great suspicion. Since they may have no contact with British families, their only sources of information about British society and its values are often television, the press and advertisements. Their suspicion is confirmed when they see the rates of divorce and illegitimacy, and the sexual freedom of the young. Many parents fear for their children's happiness in case they pick up what they see as British values.

They also feel that the western family has no time or room for its old people. Parents may fear that if their children make 'love marriages' the whole family will break up and there will be no place for them when they are old. To counteract this, Asian parents may demand higher standards of behaviour and decorum from their children.

At the same time, their children at school are being taught very different ideas about personal responsibility and individual choice. As part of this, most young people in Britain go through a whole series of temporary relationships which, it is believed, will enable them to judge wisely when the time comes to choose a permanent partner. This process of trial and error is interpreted by many Asian parents purely as sexual licence. They feel that parents who let their children get into such moral danger cannot love them.

The conflict between the two cultures becomes really serious when the children reach marriageable age.

Marriage is traditionally the time, most of all, when a young person must trust the judgment and love of his family, and accept its wisdom in choosing the marriage partner. Young Asians growing up in Britain, on the other hand, learn to see marriage as one of the most important *independent* decisions they will ever have to make. It is a decision in which they are expected to consider their own wishes and needs above all other considerations, and in which other people should not interfere.

It is *now* that compromise may seem impossible. Do they accept the partner their parents have chosen, or do they refuse and risk cutting themselves off from their family and from the Asian community?

For the parents, the decision may be further complicated by other factors.

Since the different Asian communities are far more scattered in Britain than they are in the subcontinent, there is not the same network of relatives to investigate the prospective partner and report on his or her character and suitability. Parents may not know the partner they choose nearly as well as they would have done at home.

Some parents may attempt to ensure the unity of their family in Britain and to strengthen their own deeply held beliefs and values by bringing in a marriage partner from the home country. This was the usual practice among Asian communities in East Africa. Many parents in India are also very keen to send their children to Britain to marry, as they feel that this ensures a better life and greater opportunities. These pressures may distort the normal processes of choosing marriage partners. There are bound to be differences between husband and wife, of experience, education, expectations and values, particularly when the husband comes from the subcontinent. The pressures of adjustment and of very different expectations may make such marriages unhappy.

Life may be particularly difficult for the wife, who traditionally must obey her husband, and who is less likely to have interests outside her home.

On the whole, however, most young Asians are bound to their families by strong and lasting love, from which they might be cut off if they refused to trust their parents' judgment. They feel close enough to their families and to their cultural roots to let their parents choose a partner for them and to work at developing the relationship within the arranged marriage.

Old people

Among Asians from the Indian subcontinent there are at present relatively few old people. There is a much larger proportion among immigrants from East Africa, many of whom were forced by circumstances beyond their control to leave their homes and to come to Britain. Many have undergone a tremendous drop in standard of living and in status. The whole experience may have been traumatic. They are often too old to change and have not had time to learn about or understand the new culture.

Elderly Asians share many of the problems of elderly Britons: financial insecurity, housing problems, loneliness, decreasing mobility and failing health. In addition, their position in the family has often changed dramatically. Traditionally, the elderly are revered and receive physical and emotional support. They have a good deal of power. They are not expected to be active or to work, even around the house. Their financial and physical dependence is accepted. Senility and incontinence, for example, which a British family may find difficult, are accepted and contained within the extended Asian family. No family would consider putting old people into a home or a geriatric ward. In Britain, most Asian families still look after their elderly even though this may become a real burden.

In some cases, however, instead of being the wisest and most respected members of the family, the elderly may be rejected as being out of touch. If money is tight, their financial dependence often brings strains. They may also be resented where a family has inadequate housing.

Local authority and government provision often does not cater for the needs of elderly Asians. For example, the food provided by meals-on-wheels or luncheon clubs, and the activities of day centres, are not usually suitable for them. There are very few places where elderly members of the Asian community can meet and spend their days undisturbed and unrestricted.

There are likely to be significant numbers of elderly people in most East African Asian communities who have come to Britain with no family or relatives, and for them the problems of living in Britain are particularly stark.

4 Religion

Most Asian immigrants come from societies where religion is a natural part of life. There is no distinction between religious observance and daily routine. Everything has a religious significance and a person judges himself and others accordingly. Many immigrants find the secular society of Britain difficult to understand.

The three major religions among Asian immigrants in Britain are Hinduism, Sikhism and Islam (see Figure 1, page 6).*

Hinduism

Hinduism has no founder, no central creed and no central administrative organisation or hierarchy of ministers. It has been passed down and developed in different ways by different groups in India over thousands of years. There are, however, certain common beliefs, the most important of which are non-violence and reincarnation. Hinduism is very tolerant of differences within itself, and of other religions.

---

* Only the main points of the three religions are mentioned in this chapter. More detailed information of special importance to health workers is given in the following chapters throughout the book.

One, largely Gujarati, sect, with members in Britain, is the Swami Narayan sect founded in the nineteenth century. There are sizeable Swami Narayan communities in Bolton and in North London.

God

Hindus believe that there is one God, who can be understood and worshipped in many different forms. The three most important manifestations are Brahma (the creative power), Vishnu (the preserver) and Shiva (the destroyer). There are many other manifestations which stress the different qualities of God and are worshipped by different groups; for example, Lord Krishna, Lord Rama, Ganesha.

Duty

Every Hindu should pray, revere the old, and offer food and generous hospitality to any visitor. In addition to the belief in non-violence, Hindus refuse to take life, and most are vegetarians.*

Hindu women are responsible for the religious education of children, for performing many of the family's religious obligations and often for leading the family in prayer. The status of women is generally high.

Great stress is placed on the importance of the family and on the duties and roles of the different family members. The role of the older members is to advise and rule; that of younger people is to respect, listen, obey and learn.

* See Chapter 11, Food, pages 121–145.

There are also responsibilities and duties that go with one's position in society. Everyone has certain clear duties depending on his circumstances and social position.

Reincarnation

Man is caught up in a cycle of birth and rebirth. Each person must try to live such a good life that he rises above the cycle of rebirth and becomes one with God. Until he does so, he is bound to be reborn again and again. In each new life, his status and condition are determined by his behaviour in his last life. Each person is, therefore, responsible for who he is and what he does.

Caste

The caste system is closely linked to the theory of reincarnation. Everyone is born into the caste for which his behaviour in his past life has fitted him. Members of each caste have a certain role in society and certain duties to perform. They must not perform the duties of someone in a different caste.

In many ways the caste system has been harmful to Indian society, making it static and conservative. Nowadays, however, with increasing urbanisation and social movement, people's views are becoming less rigid. The Indian government has brought in laws against caste discrimination. It will, nevertheless, take a long time to eradicate values and social traditions which have a religious sanction and have been established over many centuries.

There are four major castes

Brahmins   priests and teachers

Kshatriyas   warriors and rulers

Vaishyas   farmers, merchants and craftsmen

Shudras   manual workers and servants

There is also a fifth group, the Outcastes, who have duties which are traditionally regarded as polluting, such as cleaning lavatories, streets and other public areas, and touching the flesh of dead animals.

The castes also vary in how strictly they follow dietary laws, the forms of prayer required and ritual purification.

The most orthodox and conservative Hindus, those who would be expected to stick most rigidly to concepts of caste pollution and purification, do not usually emigrate.

Most of the Hindus in Britain belong to the same caste and only a few subcastes. There is, therefore, little variation in the duties required of them. Restrictions on occupation have also become largely irrelevant in Britain. However, caste differences are still likely to have an important effect on social behaviour and on how people feel about their place in society.

Subcastes

Each caste contains a great many subcastes. Each subcaste is made up of a small group of people, all of whom come from one social and occupational group, and from one small geographical area. Hindus can generally recognise each other's subcastes from their surnames or subcaste names. For example, Patel indicates a member of the Patidar subcaste.*

* See Chapter 8, Names, pages 87–104.

Subcastes operate in many ways like a caste. All the members usually worship in the same way, have the same fundamental beliefs and are traditionally associated with certain occupations. Each subcaste is, therefore, a cohesive social group with common values, customs and tastes.

People generally regard their own subcaste as a large kin-group with whom they feel at ease and to whom they may have certain obligations. They mix socially within their own subcaste, and most Hindu marriages are arranged strictly within subcaste groups. In many ways subcastes resemble the rather rigid and exclusive social groups of the British class system and often operate in the same way.

Most Asian children in Britain do not grow up with an instinctive understanding of, or respect for, caste and subcaste divisions, and the force of these divisions is therefore diminishing. However, many parents still feel it is important for their children to make friends within their own subcaste.

It is interesting to note that immigrants from India and East Africa, who belong to the same caste and subcaste, do not generally mix socially and marriages between members of the two groups are unusual.

Worship

Spiritual devotion and worship are usually individual rather than communal. Many Hindus, particularly women, visit the temple for private prayer at least once a day. Many Hindu families visit the temple on Sunday. Each temple has a priest. His duties are chiefly religious rather than pastoral.

Most Hindus pray at least once a day, at sunrise. They must wash thoroughly and change their clothes before praying.

Many households have a family shrine with pictures of deities at which the family may worship together, particularly in the evenings. A room set aside for a shrine should not be entered without an invitation, and should be treated as a holy place. Everyone must remove shoes before entering.

In hospital, patients may have the picture of God or a copy of the Bhagvad Gita (the most popular Hindu holy book) on their locker. Religious comfort is likely to be offered by family or friends and not by a priest.

Jainism

Jainism was founded as an offshoot of Hinduism in the sixth century BC. Jains are not Hindus, but they have lived side by side with Hindus for many centuries and their beliefs and ideas have been influenced by Hinduism. In Britain they may describe themselves as Hindus and may attend Hindu temples. Almost all of the small number of Jains in Britain are Gujarati in origin, though some have come from East Africa, where they formed prosperous communities. Many Jains have the subcaste name of Jain or Shah (but not all people with the subcaste name, Shah, are Jains).*

The central doctrine of Jainism is respect for life. In India, strict Jains sweep the ground in front of them to avoid stepping on any living thing. Most Jains, especially women, are extremely strict vegetarians. They may refuse any food that has been cooked in utensils that have been used for meat. Many Jains also avoid 'hot' foods[†], and may fast on one or two days a week.

* See also Chapter 8, Names, pages 87–104.
† See also Chapter 11, Food, pages 121–145.

Festivals

Mahashivratri　　birthday of Lord Shiva. A fast day, followed by celebrations at night (March).

Holi　　five-day spring festival (March).

Ram Naumi　　birthday of Lord Rama. A fast day, followed by celebrations at night (April).

Raksha Bandhan　　celebration of the bond between brothers and sisters, when brothers promise to protect their sisters all their lives wherever they may be (July/August).

Jan Mash Tami　　birthday of Lord Krishna. A fast day, with celebrations day and night (end of August).

Navratri　　festival of Goddess Ambaji. Prayer, singing, dancing. Particularly a Gujarati festival (October).

Dassera　　commemorates Lord Rama. An Indian national festival with day-long celebrations (October).

Diwali　　festival of light, associated present-giving and family celebration (October/November).

Bestuvarash/Nutanvash　　new year's day, the day after Diwali (October/November).

The two most important festivals are Holi and Diwali. Dates of all festivals vary from year to year. Some are celebrated on the nearest Saturday or Sunday by Hindus in Britain.

Note: **Most community relations councils can supply a list of festival dates for the current year for Hinduism, and for Sikhism and Islam.**

Sikhism

All Sikhs are Punjabi in origin. Most of the Sikhs in Britain come direct from Punjab, though there are a few from East Africa.

Sikhism developed as a reformist movement of Hinduism in the sixteenth century. The founder, Guru Nanak, was greatly opposed to the various excesses of his time such as idolatry, ostentatious and elaborate worship, strife between Hindus and Moslems, and the evils of the caste system. He tried to combine the best features of Hinduism and Islam. He stressed the equality of all men, and the importance of practical devotion and right action rather than religious rites and theological speculation.

There was a succession of ten Sikh gurus in all. They are revered as saints but not worshipped. During the early period, Sikhs were persecuted by the Mogul emperors and developed strong traditions of brotherhood and unity which remain most important.

God

Sikhs believe in one God and, unlike Hindus, do not worship different manifestations of God. Man's duty is to learn about God by looking at the world he has created and so to become more like him. Every Sikh aims to reach true understanding and unity with God after many cycles of birth and rebirth.

Duties

There are very few practical regulations covering the everyday or religious activities of Sikhs. Every Sikh makes his own relationship with God and worships in his own way. Sikhism emphasises the practical rather than the theoretical. Every Sikh has a duty to be useful to the community: to marry, to raise a family and to participate in community affairs.

Sikh women are highly respected and have great influence in important domestic and community matters. Both men and women take part in all important religious ceremonies. Women are educated equally with the men and have a good deal of freedom and authority, though, as among Hindus and Moslems, there is a system of etiquette which influences behaviour between the sexes in public.

Some Sikhs have chosen to undergo a kind of confirmation and have 'taken Amrit'. Amritdari Sikhs are bound to observe special rules: to attend the Gurdwara (temple) every day, to say special prayers, to wear the five signs of Sikhism (see below), to eat no meat nor anything of which another person has already eaten a part.*

Sikhism preaches the equality of all people, irrespective of caste or other differences. In practice, however, caste-consciousness still influences Sikhs, since they were mostly originally converted from Hindu families, and have continued to live within the mainly Hindu culture of the Indian subcontinent. Caste is chiefly important in marriage. However, other aspects of Sikhism reinforce the eradication of other features of the caste system: for example, every Gurdwara contains a communal kitchen. This is a clear rejection of the Hindu restrictions on different castes eating together.

At the end of the seventeenth century, the tenth and last guru, Guru Gobind Singh, wished to strike a final blow to the caste system among his followers. He instituted the Sikh naming system in which the last (subcaste) name was dropped and the first (personal) name was used, with a religious second (or complementary) name: *Singh* (male) and *Kaur* (female). †

* See also Chapter 11, Food, pages 121–145.
† See also Chapter 8, Names, pages 87–104.

The five signs of Sikhism

Guru Gobind Singh also provided five easily identifiable features by which all Sikhs might recognise each other.

uncut hair on head and body (men and women)

a comb to secure the hair on the head, worn by men under the turban

a metal bangle, kara, worn on the right wrist (men and women)

a special martial undergarment (men)

a small symbolic dagger, kirpan, (men and women).

The most important is the metal bangle; this must never be removed. Some people wear the symbolic dagger as a brooch or pendant.*

Worship

The centre of a Sikh community is the Gurdwara. Communal worship is important, and in Britain the Gurdwara is a community meeting place and family centre. Most families try to go there on a Sunday. Devout Sikhs, particularly women, may go early every morning to pray. Every Gurdwara has an elected reader or caretaker called the Granti.

Most large Gurdwaras are always open to provide shelter and food for any Sikh in need or on a visit. Some Gurdwaras in Britain also provide facilities for the elderly and other groups. Before going into the Gurdwara, everybody must remove shoes and cover the

* See also Jewellery, pages 116–118.

head. On special occasions and on Sundays, a full-scale meal is contributed, cooked and served to members of the community.

Every Sikh must say certain prayers morning and evening. These can be said anywhere. Some Sikh families gather each morning before the Guru Grant Sahab (holy book) for a short reading. Though communal prayer at the Gurdwara is important, there is also a good deal of emphasis on silent private prayer.

The Guru Grant Sahab is a collection of writings of the ten gurus. The tenth guru, Guru Gobind Singh, commanded that there should be no gurus after him, and that from his time on, the Sikhs should use the Guru Grant Sahab as their teacher.

Festivals

Birthday of Guru Gobind Singh   the tenth and last guru (18 January).

Holi   five-day spring festival. Family celebration (March).

Baisakhi   (also known as Amrit Parchar)   new year's day, commemorates the founding of the Sikh religion, with prayer, songs and processions. It is also the spring harvest festival in Punjab (13 April).

Martyrdom of Guru Arjan Dev   the fifth guru, in 1606 (June).

Rakhi   (Hindu: Raksha Bandhan)   celebration of the bond between brothers and sisters, when brothers promise to protect their sisters all their lives wherever they may be (July/August).

Dassera   commemorates Lord Rama. An Indian national festival with day-long celebrations (October).

Diwali   festival of light, associated with present-giving and family celebration (October/November—the date may vary by one or two days from that on which Hindus celebrate Diwali).

Birthday of Guru Nanak   the founder of Sikhism. Prayer and celebration with fireworks (November/December).

Martyrdom of Guru Tegh Bahadur   the ninth guru. Procession, celebration and prayer (December).

The most important festivals are Baisakhi and Diwali, the latter and some others being shared with Hinduism. Most dates vary from year to year, and some festivals are celebrated on the nearest Saturday or Sunday by Sikhs in Britain.

Islam

Islam was founded at the beginning of the seventh century by the prophet Mohammed, who was born and lived in Saudi Arabia. Within a few decades of his death, Islam had spread as far west as Spain and as far east as Eastern India.

The prophet Mohammed laid down very specific rules, which were given to him by God, about the spiritual, physical and community life of Moslems, and which are written in the holy book of Islam, the Koran. There is, therefore, a great deal of similarity in practices and beliefs of Moslems all over the world.

God

Moslems believe in one God, known by the Arabic name, Allah, the Eternal Omnipotent Creator of the universe and of man, the Compassionate and the Merciful. Moslems believe that Mohammed was the last and the most important in a long line of prophets, including Noah, Abraham, Moses and Jesus, sent by God to teach right living to mankind. Mohammed was careful to state very clearly that he was only a messenger from God, an instrument to proclaim Allah's will, and that he was not to be seen as a mediator between man and God.

Man is to live on earth as perfectly as he can. When he dies he will be judged by God, and rewarded or punished for his earthly life in the life hereafter. Every man is accountable to God for all that he does on earth.

Duties

There are five main duties, known as the 'pillars' of Islam, which every Moslem must follow.

Faith   in God, and in Mohammed as his prophet. God is the creator from whom life comes and to whom it returns. Only God is to be worshipped.

Prayer   All Moslems must pray formally five times a day: before sunrise, in the early and late afternoon, just after sunset and during the night. The prescribed prayers vary in length. A Moslem may pray anywhere as long as he is physically clean and is praying on clean ground. A mat is usually used. There is a ritual procedure for washing, and prayers must be said with the head towards Mecca (southeast in Britain), and the forehead must touch the ground. Moslems in this country may try to fit their prayers into convenient moments of the day, but the ritual washing is extremely important.

Friday is the Moslem holy day. Prayer on that day is the most important, and all men should go to the mosque for congregational prayer.

Women, except for the members of one small sect (the Ismailis), do not go to the mosque for public prayer. They usually pray alone at home. When people are ill they may pray silently in bed provided that they are clean. Moslems may use prayer beads in the same way as Roman Catholics use a rosary.

Fasting All Moslems, except those specially exempted*, must fast throughout the day during Ramazan.[†] This is the ninth lunar month, when they enter into poverty and practise self-discipline and when prayer is particularly important.

Charity The Koran lays down the amount of money which every Moslem must give to the poor each year. Most Moslem communities also have to give further sums of money for other charities and for the upkeep of buildings.

Pilgrimage Every Moslem man and woman who is able, must go on a pilgrimage to Mecca, the holy city of Islam, at least once during life. The pilgrimage should be made during the twelfth month of the Islamic year; before the pilgrimage, the financial security of the family left behind must be ensured. Anyone who has made the pilgrimage may add Hajji (Hadji, Al Hajj) to his name and is entitled to great respect in the community.

Islam contains a very clearly defined moral and practical code governing religious observance, daily behaviour, eating habits, clothing, marriage, divorce, inheritance, finance, the family, hospitality, law and politics. This code was passed down to man through the prophet Mohammed, and is followed by Moslems all over the world.

Islam emphasises the equality of all people regardless of race, status or nationality, and is fundamentally opposed to caste.

* See also Chapter 11, Food, pages 121–145.
[†] Often spelt and pronounced Ramadan in Britain.

However, in the Indian subcontinent, where most Moslems are the descendants of people converted from Hinduism many centuries ago, and where Hindus and Moslems have continued to live side by side, some of the attitudes of the caste system have remained, particularly with regard to marriage, social status and traditional occupations.

The Mosque

Most Moslem communities in Britain have a local mosque where services and classes are held. It is the centre of male religious and community life. There will be an Imam who reads the Koran and leads prayers, and who will also be concerned with the well-being of the community and with teaching the children to read the Koran. As a 'community centre' in the British sense, the mosque can be a useful means for health workers to contact the community and to publicise health care facilities or community projects.

The Koran

The Koran is the direct word of Allah dictated through the mouth of his prophet, Mohammed. The Koran may not be placed under any other book. It should be the highest thing in a room. It must not be touched by anyone who is not ritually clean or by a non-Moslem. No one may talk, smoke or eat while it is being read, and both men and women should cover their heads.

Copies of the Koran in a mosque must always be in Arabic and it is not considered that any translation of the Koran can be really accurate. Thus, every Moslem should learn Arabic in order to read the Koran. Many Moslem children in Britain go to the mosque school in the evenings or at weekends to read and study the Koran. Some Moslems may wear verses of the Koran in a locket or pouch to protect them from misfortune.

45

Women

Under Islamic law, the differences between the roles and duties of men and of women are made very clear. The rights of women, however, are in many cases equal to those of men, though some women, in practice, are treated as inferiors. The Koran specifies, for example, that men and women should be educated equally. The Koran also states that women should be protected and respected by men.

The prophet Mohammed attempted to protect the women of his time by introducing purdah, physical seclusion. Women should veil themselves outside their own homes and should not meet any men except very close relations. According to custom, a man who cares for his wife, and protects her by keeping her away from contact with crowds and strange men, is a good husband. The observation of purdah has, therefore, become a sign of high status and is something which many poorer people aspire to.

A Moslem woman is always under the guardianship of a man: her father, husband, or sons if she is a widow. This is chiefly important in matters concerning the outside world. In the family, men and women generally share in making decisions. There is, however, a rigid formal code of public behaviour between the sexes. This should not be mistaken as indicating the real relationships within a family.

In Islamic law, physical contact between a woman and a man who is not her husband is forbidden. For this reason, some women will react strongly against, for example, physical examination by a male doctor, or male ambulance drivers coming into the home.

Marriage and divorce

Marriage is a civil contract, not a sacrament. Islam allows men to have four wives, but national legislation throughout the Indian subcontinent prohibits polygamy except in certain cases; for example, where the wife cannot bear children or where she is mentally ill. It is rare for Moslem husbands from the Indian subcontinent to have more than one wife.

Divorce is permitted but is frowned upon and the local community will do all it can to prevent a divorce. When it occurs, it is usually initiated by the man. The children of divorced parents may be raised by the mother until they are seven, but they are under the guardianship of their father. Divorced or widowed men and women are encouraged to remarry.

Circumcision

Moslem boys must be circumcised before puberty. In some hospitals in Britain this is done by a Jewish minister; elsewhere it may be done by the family doctor.

Hygiene

The left hand has negative connotations; only the left hand may be used for washing the body after using the lavatory. The right hand is always used for eating, shaking hands, pointing and so on. This can cause difficulties when Moslems become patients in British hospitals or have other contacts with GPs and community health services.

Sects

There are two major sects: the Sunni Moslems and the Shia Moslems. Within these two are further divisions into smaller sects. Some are more conservative than others, and each sect usually worships and socialises separately and has its own central authority. The practical and religious code of Islam outlined above is, however, generally followed.

Festivals

The dates of Moslem festivals are based on the lunar calendar (12 months of 28 days each). Most festivals depend on the siting of the moon and dates may therefore vary from area to area and from country to country. Some of the less important festivals are celebrated on the nearest Saturday or Sunday in Britain.

Birthday of the Prophet Mohammed

Lailat Ul-Mi'raj   journey of the prophet Mohammed to heaven.

Lailat Ul-Bara'at/Shab-i-Bharat   congregational prayer to atone for past wrongs and to pray for the future.

Ramazan   obligatory fast from all foods and liquids between dawn and sunset for 30 days, compulsory prayers during the day, including one at midday and one during the afternoon.

Eed-ul-Fitr   marks the end of Ramazan with great celebration, feasting and exchange of presents.

Eed-ul-Azha/Adha/Zuha   commemorates the willingness of Abraham to sacrifice Isaac at God's command, and celebrates the prophet Mohammed's pilgrimage to Mecca.

Muharram   commemorates the death of the prophet's grandson, Husain, in a battle.

Dates of Ramazan and Eed-ul-Azha

Islamic year	AD year	Ramazan begins	Eed-ul-Azha/Zuha
1399	1979	26 July	1 November
1400	1980	14 July	20 October
1401	1981	4 July	9 October
1402	1982	24 June	30 September
1403	1983	13 June	20 September
1404	1984	2 June	9 September
1405	1985	22 May	29 August

Funeral rites and practices

In British culture, mourning is usually a private affair. Public display of grief is embarrassing; restrained behaviour is expected and admired. Asian attitudes to dying and death are very different. Display of strong emotion is considered natural, praiseworthy and healthy. The whole family, however scattered it may be, comes together to show its grief, to talk freely about the dead member and to concentrate upon the loss. A period of unconcealed sorrow is considered necessary to heal the grief. A newly widowed Asian woman, for example, is not expected to be 'brave' and control her feelings. All her relatives have a binding obligation to visit her and to share in the mourning, and she is expected to ask for their help and support.

In the subcontinent, burial or cremation must be arranged as soon as possible after a death. In the hot climate, decay sets in quickly. All rites and duties are organised and performed by the family, if possible at home. This includes washing and laying out the body—an important part of the mourning process. The British custom of having undertakers is quite foreign to Asians. They may find the involvement of such people, mortuary staff or indeed anyone not personally concerned, intrusive and upsetting. Distressing incidents have occurred in hospitals where the authorities did not consider it suitable for relatives to see a body. In one case, as Asian woman who had given birth to a stillborn child was considered to be behaving morbidly and was sedated when she wished to see the body and dress it for cremation.

The close and active involvement of the family is common to all Asian groups, though the rites and duties vary according to the requirements of the different religions.

Hindus

When a Hindu is dying, a priest or a member of the family will pray, sing hymns or read chapters from the Bhagvad Gita (the Hindu holy book) beside the bed. Sometimes the priest ties a thread around the neck or wrist of the dying person while he prays. After death, the men or women of the family usually wash the body. Many Hindus are very particular about who touches the body. It is important, therefore, to ask the family about this when a Hindu dies in hospital.

Hindus are usually cremated. Children may be buried. The body is wrapped in a white cotton shroud and is taken, usually by the men, for cremation. There may be a special service beforehand, usually at home, but, in Britain, it may be held at the chapel of rest. It is the sacred duty of the eldest son to light the funeral pyre. During the cremation more prayers are chanted. When the body is completely burnt the ashes are collected in a jar and may be sent home to be scattered in the River Ganges.

For ten days after the funeral, white clothes may be worn as a sign of mourning. The family says special prayers and eats only simple food. The widow and eldest son of the dead man may shave their heads.

There is no religious prohibition against autopsy.

Sikhs

A devout Sikh who is very ill or dying receives comfort from reciting hymns from Guru Grant Sahab (the Sikh holy book). If he is so near death that he cannot recite the hymns himself, the family or a reader from the Sikh temple may read them instead.

Sikhs cremate the body. It is washed and dressed with the five symbols of Sikhism and wrapped in a white cotton shroud. The whole family prays beside the body and there are hymns and readings from the Guru Grant Sahab. After cremation the ashes are collected and scattered in the sea or sent home to be buried or scattered there. In Britain there is generally a short service at the Gurdwara (Sikh temple) after the cremation.

There is usually no religious prohibition against autopsy.

Moslems

When a Moslem is very ill or dying, a member of the family often recites the Koran by the bedside. At the time of death the person should sit or be facing Mecca; another Moslem, usually a member of the family, must whisper the call to prayer into the dying person's ear.

According to Islamic law, Moslems must be buried within 24 hours of death. The body is first taken home and bathed by the men or women of the family. It is wrapped in a white shroud (called a 'kaffan'), while the family prays. Then the men take the body to the mosque or to the graveside for further prayers before it is buried.

In Britain it is not always possible to follow the rules laid down in the Koran for burials, and many Moslem families prefer to take their dead home to be buried. This requires an extremely complicated bureaucratic procedure and can be very distressing.

Moslems may not be buried in a coffin. According to Islamic law, the area above the grave must be slightly raised, the body must be buried facing Mecca and the grave must be unmarked. Except in the very few Moslem cemeteries in Britain, this is often against local cemetery regulations. The grave is usually visited every Friday for 40 days after the funeral. Alms are given to the poor.

According to Islam, a Moslem is not the owner of his body and, therefore, no part of a dead body should be cut out, harmed or donated to anyone else. Post-mortem examination should be avoided unless absolutely necessary. If a post-mortem is necessary, the reasons must be clearly explained to the family. Moslems must not be cremated.

5 Sickness and health

Expectations

There is no general practice system in the Indian subcontinent. Patients who can afford to pay consult a private doctor; others go directly to a hospital, which is usually free. It may take time for Asian patients in Britain to understand the hospital referral system.

Few hospital and medical facilities in the subcontinent are equal in scope and standards to those in Britain. In some more prosperous areas, however, there is a hospital in every town, though beds, equipment and treatment may be limited, and standards of hygiene and care are generally lower. Only the very seriously ill are admitted. People rarely, if ever, go in for observation, checkups, minor operations or childbirth. Even so, most hospitals are severely overcrowded.

Some of the more prosperous areas also have government health centres in the larger villages, with female health visitors or medically trained health officers whose role is often preventive and educational.

In poorer, less developed areas, medical facilities are generally few and far between. Many people cannot afford any treatment at all, and those who can may have to travel many miles to get it.

53

Again, only patients who are very seriously ill are admitted to hospital. Many Asians from these areas may never have been inside a hospital.

For many people from the subcontinent, therefore, hospitals conjure up ideas of serious or fatal illness, and are extremely frightening. Many people have no idea what goes on inside a hospital in Britain. They are likely to be further confused if they speak little or no English.

Illness in the Indian subcontinent

Because of the scarcity of medical provision, many complaints that would be quickly cured in Britain are serious or incurable in the subcontinent. As a result, both major and minor illnesses are often regarded more seriously and with greater fear. In a tropical climate, for example, even a chill or a slight temperature may lead to pneumonia, and small cuts quickly become infected. Infections that in Britain would be considered minor and easily curable may do lasting damage.

A woman in childbirth is still, in a real sense, risking death. If she survives, she is often regarded as having been granted a new life. Infant and child mortality rates are high. Facts such as these are bound to affect the behaviour and fears of many patients from the Indian subcontinent.

People from rural areas may also have had little health education, and may not understand much about the causes of disease and pain. Some Asian patients also have misconceptions about anatomy and physiology, and believe firmly in the curative powers of certain rituals and in the power of the 'evil eye'.

Various Asian practices conflict with British customs. People do not usually take cold drinks when they are ill as these are believed to cool the body dangerously. They usually wrap up well, and take only hot drinks. They may be afraid that bathing when ill, particularly in a cold climate, may cause chills or pneumonia. They may believe that it is very important to stay in bed for as long as possible after childbirth or a surgical operation. Many Asian patients, therefore, may be worried by British hospital practices, which are often very different from those they are used to, and which they feel must be bad for them.

Preventive medicine and provision of free and regular medical checkups are also new to many Asians in Britain. Few people are likely to go regularly for smear tests or dental treatment unless the importance of doing so has been clearly demonstrated.

Hospitals in East Africa

Most Asians from East Africa have come from cities or small towns where hospital facilities were readily available. Some of the Asian communities, depending on their collective wealth, ran fee-paying hospitals for their own members before the East African countries became independent. Since independence, these have been opened to the general public. There were also free government hospitals in East Africa though these tended to be overcrowded and poorly equipped. People who could afford it preferred to go to a fee-paying hospital. Most Asian women in East Africa had their babies in hospital.

East African Asian patients are, therefore, likely to be more familiar with hospital procedures (queues, registration, record cards, prescriptions), and far less intimidated or frightened in hospital in Britain.

The fee-paying hospitals in East Africa placed a good deal of emphasis on personal service by nurses and ward orderlies.

So, while most East African Asians appreciate the standards of medical care in British hospitals, they may also expect more personal service and attention than they are likely to receive.

Asian patients in British hospitals

When working with individual patients, it is clearly not useful to exaggerate the differences caused by culture or geography. A sick child and a worried patient are a sick child and a worried patient, wherever they come from. Anxiety, impatience, dependence and depression are common to all sick people. The behaviour of each patient, and the ability to cope with illness, depend largely upon individual character and circumstances.

Many of the problems that Asian patients encounter in Britain arise because the British hospital system is very different from anything many of them have met before. Routine and practical details are unfamiliar. And, like many British patients, Asians may not understand who is who and who is responsible for what on the ward.

The loneliness and vulnerability become worse if patients cannot speak English. They will be treated and attended by people who cannot explain what they are doing or what is going to happen next. They may become extremely distressed--to the point of panic.

Someone who speaks the patient's language should be at hand to explain what is happening, to answer questions and to discuss any fears or worries. It is also most important to pay as much attention to patients who cannot speak English as to those who can. Hospital staff are sometimes reluctant to go over to a patient except on business if they cannot speak to him. He may interpret this as dislike or discrimination.

Behaviour in illness

In Britain, a person who suffers but hides his suffering is respected. In hospital, patients are expected to remain cheerful, to behave 'normally', and to cope with their fears and worries as far as possible on their own. It is considered unhealthy for sick people to dwell on their fears or talk about them too much. They are expected not to make too many demands on others. Often, only the immediate family and close friends will disturb a sick person's privacy by visiting him. They usually try to avoid intruding on, or letting him dwell on, his suffering.

Acceptable behaviour in times of sickness is very different in Asia. A sick person who behaves in the way that is generally admired in Britain may be thought odd. Other people will not take his illness seriously. He is not expected to carry on as normal, or to be active and cheerful. He should let his illness take its physical and emotional course. He should go to bed and stay there until he gets better. It is considered natural for the sick to express anxiety and suffering. Asian patients may cry and moan in a way that upsets the other patients in a British hospital ward. They are unlikely to realise that they are disturbing other people. Concepts of active rehabilitation and exercise are new to most people from the Indian subcontinent.

It is, therefore, important to remember that behaviour which might have one interpretation with a British patient, may require a different interpretation in an Asian patient.

Doctors

Doctors are generally greatly respected. However, despite the high status accorded to them, they are also expected to develop a personal relationship with their patients.

Most Asians in Britain are used to having to pay for medical treatment. In a fee-paying system, though patients are dependent upon the medical skills of doctors and other medical staff, the doctor is dependent for his livelihood on retaining the confidence of his patients. They are likely to be influenced by such factors as his reputation and manner, and by his ability to convey competence and personal concern. Few people will come a second time to see a doctor who seems unconcerned, or who tells them to come back in a few weeks if their symptoms have not cleared up.

Asian patients may, therefore, be worried by the less personal style of health provision in Britain. Some, particularly East African Asians, may be upset, for example, by the short and infrequent visits of doctors to the wards. When they compare this with what happened at home, they may feel that they are not getting their fair share of attention or treatment. Some Asian patients prefer to seek out a doctor with a good reputation and attend him privately, since they feel that this will ensure greater attention and a better standard of care.

Many Asians in Britain have registered with Asian doctors. This solves the language problem and helps the doctor to get accurate descriptions of symptoms. A close link between Asian doctors and the Asian communities also helps in matters such as health education and preventive screening. Asian doctors are widely used by the Asian communities as sources of advice on non-medical problems they encounter in Britain, particularly in the early days of immigration.

But very few Asian doctors in Britain come from the same areas or backgrounds of the Asian immigrant patients. Many are also very westernised in outlook and inclination. There are, therefore, likely to be differences of language, 'class' and culture between some Asian doctors and their patients. An Asian doctor will not necessarily understand or identify with his Asian patients any more easily than a British doctor will. Allocating all patients from the subcontinent to a doctor from the subcontinent may not always be beneficial to either side.

Asian women and male doctors

For some Asian women, particularly in their early years in Britain, a major factor of their fear of hospitals, and of doctors, is the possibility of having to be examined by a man. Some women do not go to surgeries or clinics, even if they think there is something wrong with them, because they are afraid that they will be seen by a male doctor. Those who *do* bring themselves to submit to examination by a male doctor may have a very strong reaction. The anguish and embarrassment of many women during a vaginal examination cannot be over-emphasised.

A woman who panics and becomes hysterical makes things extremely difficult for all those concerned with her care, and may affect her own health. Her reaction certainly interferes with the smooth and efficient running of a ward or clinic. It must, however, be accepted that her feelings are extremely strong and cannot be overcome by will power alone. Sympathy and understanding are likely to be more effective than irritation and impatience.

Asian women should be seen by female doctors whenever possible. Bookings should be made taking this into account. Where a female doctor is not available, a woman may be less ashamed if her husband is not present while she is being examined, or if the doctor is not Asian and therefore does not belong to her community, or know her family and friends. She may find it less threatening to be examined by someone who does not share her culture and her attitude to physical contact between men and women. On home visits, any examination should be made in complete privacy.

In the subcontinent and East Africa, women do not usually undress completely for examination; they uncover only one part of the body at a time. An Asian woman in Britain may be less upset if she is examined this way. Although this may cause some problems for the person performing the examination, these are likely to be outweighed by the advantages of a less distressed and more cooperative patient.

Mixed wards are obviously unsuitable for Asian patients.

Nurses

In some parts of the subcontinent, the hospital nurse is an important intermediary between doctor and patient and commands much respect. In other areas, especially among Moslems, nurses enjoy far less prestige, largely because their job involves physical contact with the opposite sex. This may affect the attitude of some Asian patients towards British nurses.

The patient's family

The extended family becomes very important in times of sickness. A sick person is expected to make demands and the family expects to play a major part in supporting and caring, and to take over the patient's normal duties and chores, so that he can take to bed and forget everything but the need to recover.

The most hospitals in the subcontinent much of the bedside care—feeding, washing, making comfortable—is performed by the patient's relatives. At least one person moves in with the patient and stays day and night. Other relatives will visit for short periods and sit, often in silence, around the patient's bed to keep him company. A mother always stays in hospital with her sick child.

The hospital is, therefore, very much a family place. The more serious the patient's condition, the more important it is for family members to be there. This explains why you may find a large number of relatives coming to see the patient on the day of his operation. A sick person is never left alone, either at home or in hospital. Anyone belonging to the family who does not visit a sick relative, is considered cold-hearted and unnatural. Visiting a relative in hospital is one of the most binding obligations.

In many hospitals in Britain, the constant presence of visitors is considered impracticable and may be upsetting to other patients. But, because of the strong cultural obligations, and because Asian families are very much aware how isolated a relative may feel in a British hospital, they are likely to feel bound to visit as often as they can. They are unlikely to understand the practical and medical reasons for restricting visiting hours, particularly when their relative is obviously lonely and depressed.

Attitudes to health and illness

Hindus, Sikhs and Moslems see the active maintenance of health as part of every man's duty. Eating the correct food and living a life free of excesses are considered important. Many Asians in Britain find that their health is affected by the change in climate, in their daily routine and in their diet. Coughs, colds and catarrh, for example, which are common in Britain, are new to many Asians. They may go to a doctor about a cold because they think he can cure it. Long hours at work and mental strain may also take a toll on health. Some people become more anxious about their health because they feel generally unwell and lacking in energy in Britain. They may worry and go to the doctor about minor complaints, particularly in their early years in this country.

Medication

Many Asian patients feel they have not received proper treatment or have not been taken seriously if they come away from the doctor without a prescription or an injection. Injections have particularly high status. Nevertheless, there may be strong resistance to continuous medication. A patient may consider himself recovered once he feels better, and may stop taking medicine or going for checkups. This is, of course, also true of many British patients. In cases where drugs have to be taken to prevent symptoms recurring, or to maintain health, a good deal of explanation and encouragement will be necessary.

Alternative Asian medicine

Western medicine is relatively new in the Indian subcontinent. But there are ancient medical remedies, some of which are being increasingly accepted in the west. In Asia, various 'alternative' doctors—for example, homoeopathic doctors, herbalists and faith healers—offer an alternative to western-style medical provision which may be scarce and expensive. In Britain, though some 'alternative' doctors charge high fees, they are often more accessible, more trusted and less alarming to Asian patients. Their advice is sought instead of, or alongside, that of orthodox doctors, particularly by older people.

Commercially produced patent medicines are also used extensively in the subcontinent—more so than in Britain—for diseases such as arthritis, rheumatism, general stomach trouble, liver complaints, headaches, listlessness, and particularly for urinogenital problems about which people are embarrassed to consult a doctor. It is important to advise patients not to take patent medicines unless the ingredients are clearly listed and are not harmful.* Some

* See also Chapter 10, Clothes, jewellery and makeup, pages 113–119.

patients may be reluctant to admit that they take patent medicines since they know that health workers may disapprove.

Attitudes to some diseases

Certain diseases, such as Hansen's disease, eczema, tuberculosis, asthma, epilepsy and all forms of mental illness, carry a deeply ingrained stigma in the Indian subcontinent. It may be generally believed that a disease is infectious, or hereditary, when it is not. Tuberculosis, which has largely lost its terror in Britain because it is known to be curable, is still greatly feared in the subcontinent. The stigma affects not only the patient but all the members of the family. Some parents will not allow their child to marry into a 'diseased' family. A serious disease in one child, therefore, may ruin the marriage chances of all the others.

As a result, some families may refuse to accept the diagnosis or try to keep the existence of the disease secret. This has implications for a health worker in, for example, the way the diagnosis is announced, and the need to be alert to the likely distress. It is also important to cooperate with a family that wishes to keep the disease secret, and to make sure that the family understands the real prognosis, which is often a good deal better than they expect.

If the Asian communities generally had more information about these diseases, the associated stigma, with all its harmful effects, might in time lose its force.

Mental and physical handicap

In many ways, the attitudes of Asians towards mental and physical handicap resemble those generally held in Britain half a century ago. They feel ashamed and guilty. They may try to keep a physically or mentally handicapped child hidden. Despite this, most

Asian families with a handicapped child are particularly caring and loving towards it. They will usually reject any idea of sending the child away from home.

Because there is very little treatment or help available in the sub-continent, Asian families in Britain may not realise that a handicapped child can often be helped by a regular programme of treatment. Some families may be over-protective.

East African families are likely to be more aware of the possibility of treatment. They are still unlikely, however, to wish to send a child away.

Sometimes, however, despite good intentions and strong feelings of duty, it may be impossible for a family to care for a child at home. There may no longer be women at home all day to share the burden of care between them. Some families may underestimate the severity of a child's handicap. Many children who would probably have died at, or soon after, birth in the subcontinent, survive as a result of treatment and care in Britain. Because of this, some families may be unprepared for the implications of a very severe handicap. They may find the support and care of a very severely handicapped child beyond them. They themselves will need a good deal of support and help, both while they are deciding what to do and afterwards.

For health workers, the language barrier causes major practical problems. It may be difficult to assess the degree of handicap, and to treat it. Parents may not understand what is being done for their child, or why, or what they should do to help. Working in two languages adds to the confusion of the physically or mentally handicapped child and of his teacher. In addition, few of the voluntary supportive associations have any experience in helping Asian families.

Mental illness

The stresses of the immigrant population may be thought likely to increase the tendency to mental illness. Asians, however, appear to form a surprisingly low proportion of psychiatric cases in Britain. The associated stigma may in itself deter people from admitting any form of mental illness in themselves or in their families.

There is very little understanding in the subcontinent of mental illness, its forms or its causes. Psychiatric hospitals are few and far between and often resemble British mental asylums of 100 years ago. There is little of the popular psychology currently in vogue in the west. Concepts such as anxiety, depression, neurosis, are not generally known. All forms and degrees of mental illness are grouped together and described by one word, 'puggāl', which can be translated as 'insane'. Admitting to mental illness, therefore, means nothing less than admitting to insanity. Most people will soldier on for as long as possible before labelling themselves 'insane'. They may become impatient with themselves and what they see as their foolishness, their sin or their lack of self-control. They may not know that most forms of mental illness are curable, or at least treatable, and they may be terrified of seeing a psychiatrist or going into hospital. As a result, they may not receive treatment until their condition is well advanced, and treatment and care become far more difficult.

Despite the fear and stigma, the families of most Asian psychiatric patients are supportive, and will often accept, for example, a permanently inactive, difficult and non-contributing member. They will generally feel he should be contained in the family, and they may be reluctant to accept outside help or to send him to hospital. On the other hand, once a professional outside the family has become involved, people's faith in western medicine may lead them to believe that a stay in hospital will automatically cure the patient, or to feel that the family has no further responsibility.

Stress and mental illness among an Asian and immigrant population, with very different priorities and values from those of the host population, may require new approaches by the health workers. More explanation and discussion than usual may be necessary.

Language is again likely to be a major problem. People will need a health worker who speaks their language, or at the very least an interpreter who also understands something of psychiatry. Without such help, it is virtually impossible to learn anything about the patient, his family, their reactions, states of mind or problems. Neighbours cannot be asked to interpret. A health worker may believe this to be practical in the short term, but it may have long-term repercussions for the patient, the family and their standing in the community.

6 Home visits

In hospital, patients and their families may feel that they are outsiders; but when a health worker visits at home, it is she who is the outsider.

Professional relationships

In western Europe, most families accept the involvement of outside professionals in their personal affairs, and both they and the professionals accept that this involvement has limits and mutual obligations. Though the relationship is friendly, it operates within limits which make it different from a normal friendship. It does not, for example, usually include the mutual exchange of presents, personal confidences, invitations to parties and weddings. A certain distance is maintained to preserve the patient's dignity and self-respect. The relationship ends when it is no longer needed.

The health worker has the right to ask certain personal questions about the patient. The patient does not have a right to ask the same questions of the health worker.

The patient is expected to tell the health worker everything that is relevant, and to follow her advice as far as possible. The health worker is not expected to involve the patient in her own personal problems, nor to make private personal demands on the patient.

These limits are understood by people who have grown up in British culture. Most can cope with, and indeed will prefer, an efficient, less personal approach. But it may feel strange and uncomfortable to newcomers to this country. The concept of a professional who 'cares' in a personal way is alien and contradictory to most people brought up in an Asian culture. They look to their family, or the kin-group, for advice or support. They do not involve outsiders in their personal affairs, nor expect them to 'care'. Some East African Asian families may find less difficulty in relating to professional health workers, depending on their experiences.

Working with the whole family

Health workers have to form a different kind of relationship with some Asian families in order to work successfully with them.

Some families may feel threatened by a visit. They feel that a professional has no part in what they consider private family matters, such as looking after their own children. They may be uncertain how much authority or legal power a health worker has, what she is looking for, or what she will report to some statutory authority. They may feel that they are being inspected.

Until these fears are answered and mutual confidence has grown, families may be unwilling to discuss matters frankly. They may fob the health worker off with smiles, trivialities and denials, and feel no obligation to follow her advice.

Alternatively, they may redefine the relationship in their own terms and treat the health worker, because of her involvement in their personal family affairs, almost as a member of the family, with all the responsibilities that go with family membership. They may make demands on her that they would make on family members or close friends. They may expect, because of her close involvement with them, an equally close involvement with her: they may give her presents, invite her to family celebrations and expect her 'caring' role to operate outside working hours. In return, they give her the affection and warmth normally reserved for family members and very close friends.

Contact with outsiders is traditionally the task of the men of an Asian family. Important decisions, even if they only affect one individual, are generally made jointly by the older members of the family, and the men in particular.

The authority structure of the family must be respected when the cooperation of family members is required. A husband is unlikely to agree to anything which has not been explained to him. A mother-in-law is unlikely to cooperate to ensure that the daughter-in-law follows instructions unless she has also been consulted. A child belongs to the whole family and not just to his parents. Everybody will be interested in what the health worker advises, and it is often possible to bring the family's influence to bear in a positive way by involving them. For older members who do not speak English, it may be necessary to bring in an interpreter.

On every visit, however, it is important to show that the elders are respected. They must be greeted first. They will judge the health worker's attitude towards them from her behaviour. Elderly people who may not be able to understand what is being said are generally extremely sensitive to being ignored.

With some families, the health worker will not be able to involve everyone and will be forced to tread a very wary path. Younger people brought up in Britain may resent some of the features of the extended family. Their reactions may affect the attitude of the whole family.

In most Asian families the rules of chaperoning are still binding. It would be most inappropriate for a male health worker to talk to an Asian girl alone, or to examine her without a chaperone.

Private, and probably forbidden, topics, such as sexual intercourse and family planning, must not be discussed with the whole family.

The 'encounter group' approach would be appalling to most Asian families. Few Asians are used to discussing and analysing their feelings and emotions with strangers.

A female worker may be mistrusted if her own dress is immodest by Asian standards. A long skirt or trousers with a long top are acceptable.

The first home visit

Unless there is a really urgent problem, it is unwise to do anything on a first visit except to establish identity and start building a relationship. Allow a good length of time for this. If the husband is not at home, leave a visiting card or a note for him. A general title such as 'nurse' may be more easily understood than 'health visitor'. It may be unwise to ask for passports as proof of identity or to find out correct names.* A passport does not necessarily help with the latter, and a family may conclude that a health worker is a representative of the law and is questioning their legal status in this country. People are most unlikely to trust or to cooperate if the relationship begins with these kinds of tensions.

In some cases, no one will open the door when a health worker calls. It is easier for a woman who cannot speak English to pretend she is not in, than to let herself be drawn into a conversation which she feels will be useless and humiliating. Some husbands are

* See Chapter 8, Names, pages 87–104.

worried that something will happen to their families while they are out at work. They may forbid their wives to open the door to anyone at all. In these cases it may again be useful to leave a note.

Conventions of hospitality

Hospitality is one of the main duties specified in all the three religions--Hinduism, Sikhism and Islam. The formalities differ from those of British hospitality.

The guest is deferred to; she is expected to ask for anything she wants or needs. Whatever is asked for must be provided. She is usually shown into the sitting room if there is one, rather than the room (often the bedroom) where the women and children spend their day. Every guest is offered something to eat and drink, though the hosts may not necessarily drink at the same time. It is good manners to accept. Children should be seen and not heard in the presence of guests. The elders of the family, if not the whole family, are there to welcome the guest. The wife will often not speak while her husband or older in-laws are there.

When the guest is someone in authority, as the health worker is often felt to be, she is treated according to particular formal rules. Nobody will tell her if she does something wrong.

7 Mothers and babies

All women have certain expectations, attitudes and fears about motherhood. Asian women are often unable to talk about them to British health workers, because of language or embarrassment. Their isolation and feelings of strangeness put them under additional strain. Despite the hospital facilities and medical expertise, many Asian women find childbirth in a British hospital a traumatic ordeal.

Most Asian girls brought up in this country, and who speak English as their first language, will not be overwhelmed, and will not require special consideration. There have been cases in which Asian girls have been referred, as a matter of routine, to special clinics for immigrant women, even though they were brought up in Britain and spoke perfect English.

Traditional expectations and practice

In the Indian subcontinent, pregnancy is still generally viewed as a time of danger and physical ill-health. Infant and maternal mortality rates are high, and death in childbirth is a very real fear. A pregnant woman needs special treatment, and as much rest and care as possible. She is not expected to be active or to stick to her usual routine, even around the house.

In Britain, Asian women are unlikely to be able to rest in the way they have been brought up to expect. Many go out to work and few have the kind of female family support they would have had at home. They worry that their health will be affected if they are not able to rest; their worry may indeed have an adverse effect on their health.

A female family affair

Pregnancy, birth and the care of infants are exclusively the business of the women of the family. A woman may not even discuss her pregnancy with her husband. She will turn to the married women in her family for instruction and guidance. They are entirely responsible for watching over and guiding her throughout, and have a good deal of authority over her. The child to be born will belong to the whole extended family. The mother is, in a sense, only one of the women concerned.

For the birth of her first and second children, a young wife usually goes back to her own family. As a daughter who has come home, she is spoilt and pampered and need not do any work. She may stay with her family from the seventh month of her pregnancy until the baby is several months old. Her husband remains in his own home.

Unless complications are expected, babies are always born at home. The only non-family member present is usually the village midwife, who attends all births. She may have had some medical training. Depending on local conditions, a government health worker may also pay an antenatal visit.

The baby is usually delivered in a special room. The midwife and the married women of the family stay with the mother during her entire labour. They hold her hands and head and bathe her brow, support and encourage her, and never leave her alone. She is not expected to make a loud noise, because she is within hearing distance of the rest of the family. During the birth, the midwife massages the mother's back. She deals with the afterbirth, cuts the cord and washes the baby immediately. She visits the new mother every day for the first couple of weeks to massage her back and stomach, wash her clothes and wash the child.

Rites and customs after birth

Immediately after the birth there are certain rites which are most important to the family. For a Moslem baby, the first sound heard must be the call to prayer whispered in its ear by a male relative. The baby must be bathed as soon as possible. In some Hindu families, the father should not see the face of his child until the rites have been performed. He or another male relative should place honey or ghee on the child's tongue. A Sikh child must have certain words from the Guru Grant Sahab (the Sikh holy book) whispered in its ear. Sometimes no new clothes are bought for a baby until it is born, to avoid tempting fate. On about the sixth day, the baby is usually given clothes and presents.

After the birth a woman must stay in bed with her baby for ten days or more. She is looked after and fed by her family. She must rest for 40 days in order to regain her strength. She is pampered and made much of. Large numbers of female visitors bring her special rich food to give her strength and promote lactation. She is 'unclean' and she does not prepare food. The clothes she and the baby wear in the early days may be regarded as polluted, and are thrown away. At the end of 40 days, she has a purifying bath, which may include reciting formal prayers and putting special herbs in the water. She cleans her room thoroughly, and she is then ready to resume her normal duties.

In East Africa

Asian families from East Africa have usually had far more exposure to western ways and medical developments. In the last 20 years, most babies have been born in hospital. Families are more accustomed to the involvement of non-family members, such as health workers, and to the procedures of antenatal and postnatal clinics. In some East African Asian communities, husbands may attend clinics with their wives and they are more likely to be involved. Despite this, many traditional attitudes have been retained.

Asian mothers in Britain

Antenatal classes

Health workers have found it very difficult to attract Asian women to antenatal classes. The notion of formal preparation for childbirth, or of non-family involvement in pregnancy, is strange to many Asian families. The language barrier may make classes quite meaningless.

In some areas, however, health workers have managed to set up classes successfully. They are usually run by a bilingual female health worker or with the help of a female interpreter. Although often slow to get started, they become popular once their reputation has spread within the local Asian community.

Certain topics, such as adaptation of the diet in Britain, shopping, keeping healthy during pregnancy and basic information about the growth of the fetus, have proved very popular. Others, such as explicit films on childbirth based on western cultural attitudes and practising complicated breathing techniques, have often proved irrelevant.

To persuade a woman to attend, it may be important to explain the classes to her whole family, and particularly to her mother-in-law, since she has so much authority.

Antenatal classes may be a useful way of making the link between a nervous mother and a health worker. This will be important during the birth, especially if it is in hospital, and afterwards, when the mother may be alone at home.

Many Asian men will feel extremely uncomfortable at an antenatal session with women present. It may be useful to set up a session just for husbands, possibly led by a male health worker.

In the maternity ward

Many Asian women arrive in hospital without knowing what will happen, and without the English to find out. Women who have not attended classes or clinics will also not have had checkups or advice on diet and health care.

Their stay in a maternity ward may be their first experience of being away from their families, and their first contact with a British institution and its routines. They may find it difficult to slot inconspicuously into the routine, and may be afraid of doing something to upset the busy efficient people in charge. They may not know anyone well enough to ask what is expected.

These problems are not confined to women having their first babies. Women who have had other children before they came to Britain may still be confused and frightened in a British maternity ward.

77

Delivery in a British hospital presents the greatest contrast to what most women from the subcontinent have been brought up to expect. Asian women in Britain have a reputation for making a lot of noise during labour. This, as we have seen, is not part of their cultural tradition. It is the result of their panic and terror.

Instead of being in her own bed surrounded by the women of her family in the privacy of her home, the woman delivers her baby in a technology-filled room attended by strangers, often men. At some stages she may even be left alone. She has no idea what will be done to her next, or what she should do, and she cannot ask. Her fears can make things difficult for the delivery team, and any frustration and irritation they may show will make things worse.

The stress can be relieved if an interpreter is present to explain what is going on. Most Asian women would also like to have a female relative, usually their mother or mother-in-law, with them during the delivery. They should be asked about this well before-hand so that arrangements can be made.

After the birth, it is extremely important to ensure that the religious ceremonies are performed.* If they are not, the relation-ship between mother and child, or husband and wife, may be affected—in extreme cases, permanently. The hospital should find out, before the delivery, through an interpreter if necessary, what the family requires and make its own regulations flexible enough to allow these ceremonies to be observed.

The Asian mother's belief that she must remain in bed will conflict with the western practice of encouraging women to get up soon after the delivery. Clear explanation of the medical advantages will usually be required. Again, an interpreter may be needed for this.

* See page 75.

In many British hospitals, it is still usual to separate the baby from the mother except for feeds and, sometimes, bathing. Asian mothers find this unnatural and cruel. By tradition, no mother ever leaves her child or even turns her back on it. Some Asian mothers may be able to accept the authority of the hospital and will allow their babies to be removed from them; others may not be prepared to allow it.

Visiting often causes problems. Asian families are used to a very different system in the subcontinent.* A husband may not feel that it is his place to visit his wife in hospital. Female relatives may come instead. They will all wish to pick it up and cuddle it, and they will bring food for the mother. Unless there are real medical reasons against these customs, they should be permitted.†

Most parents will wish to consult their family back home about the choice of a name for the new baby. This may take some time and may mean that the child is not given a real name for several weeks.

Going home with the baby

For all her troubles in hospital, an Asian mother may be very reluctant to go home soon after the birth, since she believes that a long period of rest is essential to her health. Even the light household chores which a British new mother might find accept-able and beneficial, are harmful, according to Asian tradition. A mother may also feel that she should not cook until she has had her ritual purifying bath. Women who have to go home and run a household often feel deprived and very lonely, and can become

* See Chapter 5, Sickness and health, pages 53–66.
† See Chapter 11, Food, pages 121–145.

very homesick and depressed. Some women will not leave the house during the 40 days after the birth; they will therefore miss attendance at clinics or surgeries.

A young woman living with or near her extended family will receive great emotional support. All the women will be much involved with the child, and the way it is looked after. She must follow their instruction and advice, even when they conflict directly with those of a professional health worker.

Most daughters-in-law will follow the advice of their mothers-in-law rather than that of the health visitor. The health visitor will therefore have to convince the mother-in-law. For this an interpreter is likely to be necessary. Some older women will be most reluctant to change their ideas on the care of babies. If they are antagonised, their attitudes will harden and the young mother will be placed in an impossible position. She will be caught between her duty to her family and her wish to follow the health worker's advice. The health worker may find it necessary to spend a good deal of time with the family, explaining what will benefit the baby.

An isolated mother

Many Asian women in Britain do not have older female relatives to turn to. They are likely to need a lot of help from health workers.

A mother with a first baby may have very little idea how to look after it. A young Asian girl is usually given little instruction about caring for babies. It is expected that the older women will show her what to do when the time comes, and she will learn by watching them. A young mother is also not considered capable of looking after her first baby. She may not trust her own abilities.

She may also have no access to the usual sources of information available to British new mothers, such as pamphlets, classes and neighbours. She may panic and lose her self-confidence and common sense.

A mother who has already had children in the subcontinent or East Africa may have different problems. She is likely to be disconcerted by the difference in practice and may be reluctant to take advice which conflicts with what she has done in the past.

Feeding

Breast feeding is the norm in most areas from which Asians come. Yet in Britain, surprisingly, many Asian mothers bottle feed their babies. Besides the nutritional disadvantages, this can be a health hazard. Some mothers do not fully understand mixing and sterilising procedures, or the need to keep prepared milk and food refrigerated, even in the colder climate.

Why do so many mothers bottle feed? There are various possible reasons. It is more convenient and allows mothers greater freedom. They are reluctant to breast feed without complete privacy. They feel that bottle feeding is modern and therefore better for the baby. They may believe that certain diseases—asthma and stomach troubles—can be passed through the breast milk to the baby.

Some mothers believe they should avoid certain foods and spices when breast feeding. This means cooking special dishes for themselves. They may also believe they should avoid cold drinks in case the baby catches cold. This means providing warm drinks.

Among Sikhs and Hindus it is often believed that the colostrum is harmful and might choke the baby or harm its throat. The baby may therefore not be breast fed for the first two or three days but is given sugared water. Nurses in British hospitals sometimes assume, when Asian mothers at first refuse to breast feed their babies, that they do not wish to breast feed at all, so the baby is started on a bottle régime.

Various pressures—finance, loneliness—may push a young mother back to work soon after the birth. There is no social disapproval of this after the prescribed 40 days, and women feel it is natural to return to their normal routine. They may not realise that they can start the baby off with breast feeding and change to a combination of breast and bottle when they start work again.

Weaning

In rural areas of the subcontinent, mothers wean their babies much later than western mothers would. Some babies may not be weaned until they are two years or more. Food supplements are not given while the baby is being breast fed.

Weaning is done suddenly, often by putting some unpleasant tasting substance on the nipple. The infant moves on to a little of whatever soft food the adults are eating, but without the spices. He may have a little thin dahl, rice, a chapati, semolina, biscuits and some fruit. Infants so fed may lack protein and other nutrients.

Advice on feeding

The first three principles about giving advice apply to Asians as they do to all other people. Advice is only taken

1 if the person receiving it understands why it is important

2 if it can be followed without too much difficulty

3 if it is given in terms that the person can understand.

But with Asian mothers much of your advice may have to be adapted for it to be accepted and, therefore, effective.

Although some Asian mothers will give their children food they would not eat themselves, many do not use proprietary baby foods in case the ingredients break religious dietary rules. Before recommending such foods, therefore, the list of ingredients should be examined to see if the food is suitable in this respect. Many mothers shop at Asian shops because they sell familiar goods. Asian shopkeepers might be encouraged to stock suitable proprietary brands.

It is generally more useful, however, to find out what is eaten by the adult members of the family and to base your advice on what the mother knows and can easily prepare. Many Asian dishes can be adapted for young children and it is easy for a mother preparing a meal to take out a portion for the child before she adds the spices. There is no point in teaching her to feed her children on western-style foods, however nutritious, if she does not understand them or eat them herself.

Family planning

The attitudes of most Asians to family planning reflect their traditional beliefs and customs. A family with six or seven children is considered blessed. Not all children will survive. Parents, as they grow old, have to rely entirely on their children for financial support. Motherhood is a woman's chief role and fulfilment; to be unable to bear children is a tragedy. To have no sons may be almost as bad.

These attitudes are beginning to change among Asians in Britain. Financial strain, small houses without yards or gardens, the unforeseen difficulties for a mother looking after children on her own, make a smaller family seem more desirable. It is natural, however, for these attitudes to change slowly, and that families with older members or in more conservative communities will be slowest to change.

Even a couple who have decided to use contraception may be ambivalent about their decision, torn between the traditions of their culture and the pressures of life in Britain. They may need a good deal of encouragement and support, and much careful explanation about each method of contraception. Very few couples are likely to consider contraception until they have at least one son.

Religious beliefs

There is some confusion about whether the three major religions prohibit or permit contraception, but many Asians believe it is forbidden by their religion. If a couple wish to use contraception but are doubtful about the religious ruling, it may be useful to ask a health worker of the same religion to advise them. It is possible that some people who do not wish to use contraception, but find their English inadequate to explain why to a health worker who is promoting it, will give religion as their reason for refusing.

Methods

The choice of method is mainly a personal decision. Asian women may be reluctant to take the pill because they do not like the idea of continuous medication, and because they do not want to risk thrombosis. There are also strong social and religious beliefs about menstrual bleeding*, and any method which gives rise to irregular

* See Chapter 9, Personal hygiene, pages 105–111.

bleeding is likely to be unacceptable. The cap may be totally repugnant to women who are extremely modest about their bodies, and who may not have a bathroom or some other place where it can be inserted in total privacy. It must be remembered also that many Asian women use only the left hand for contact with the genital area: it is very difficult to insert a cap with one hand.

The husband may regard contraception as his responsibility only.

Giving advice

None but the bravest of Asian women will attend a family planning clinic of her own accord. Home visits, therefore, are likely to be the only way of reaching them.

Advice should be given in the woman's own language. Otherwise it is impossible to ensure that she understands and that all her fears have been allayed. Because the whole matter is likely to be worrying, several visits may be needed, both before she actually starts using the contraceptive method, and afterwards to reassure and encourage her and to allay fears about side effects which may be alarming her.

There is generally no tradition of sex education in Asian families. A woman may know very little about anatomy, how the reproductive system works and what happens in pregnancy, even if she has had several children. If you are explaining the different methods of contraception you will need simple diagrams which she can relate easily to her own experience of her body.

She will probably have heard rumours on the dangers of the different methods: that the coil can move the heart and injure it, that anything inserted into the uterus moves to the brain, that contraception makes a woman permanently sterile, that the pill is cumulatively poisonous, or that it 'heats' the brain. It may be necessary to rule out these 'dangers' explicitly even if she does not mention them.

It is important to remember that in a traditional arranged marriage, the young couple may not be permitted to cohabit until they have spent some time getting to know each other. A 'modern' mother-in-law may send her new daughter-in-law to get advice on family planning before she has had sexual intercourse. She may be completely ignorant of what is involved and will be unable to answer any of the usual questions.

Most Asians will be embarrassed by talk of sex, and a husband and wife may be unwilling to discuss things in the presence of a third person. In many families there will be members who strongly oppose family planning of any kind. Where the husband or the older women make the decisions, it may be important to talk to them direct, and not to expect the young wife to discuss matters with them. Remember that if the older women are involved, a bilingual health worker or an interpreter will be needed.

8 Names

People in different areas of the world use different naming systems. Each has its own logic and is understood by the people who have grown up using it. The system in Britain (see Figure 3) is only one of many, but it is the one for which our record cards and other official forms are designed, and into which Asian names must be correctly slotted to avoid delays and errors.

Record clerks can cope with most British names. When a patient gives his or her name, the clerk automatically analyses what she hears, slots each part of the name into its correct space on the record card, and knows what further questions, if any, to ask. But when the clerk is faced with a different naming system, things may go seriously wrong.

Asians from the Indian subcontinent have three different naming systems, used by the three main religious groups: Hindus, Sikhs and Moslems. They are fairly easy to identify and learn, and they also serve as a guide to the patient's religion and his probable first language.

Use of names in urban and rural societies

In a closely knit village community, everybody knows everybody and there is usually little contact with administrative bureaucracy.

Figure 3 BRITISH NAMING SYSTEM

	First name (personal/Christian, different names male and female)	Middle name(s) (personal/family)	Surname (family)
female	Mary	Kathleen	Jones
male	Marcus	Edward David	Henley
female	Anne	Smith	Morrison
male	John	Smith	Morrison
	used by family and friends	used mainly in written records and on formal occasions	wife adopts husband's surname on marriage; all children of the marriage take the surname

Notes: There are many variations:

first names may be shortened (Jennifer to Jenny)

a nickname may be used instead of, or as well as, a first name or a surname

there may be several middle names which may be like first names or surnames

a middle name may be used as a first name

the surname may be two names hyphenated (Smith-Morrison)

a surname may sound like a first name (David Thomas)

Each person needs only one name, his personal name, the equivalent of our first or Christian name. If further identification is needed he may give his father's name, or a name that indicates his religion, his family or his status in the village. In many areas family names are not used in everyday dealings. Some groups, notably Moslems, do not usually have a system of family names or surnames.

In contrast, most urban industrialised societies have developed a more complex system. Individuals and families require records and legal documents. People are accustomed to using a consistent and formalised name which has a fixed order and recognised usage, as well as legal significance.

Asian groups in Britain have varying experience of urbanisation, and this affects the relative flexibility of their naming systems. In general, Moslems from Pakistan and Bangladesh have had least urban contact.

Adapting to the British system

Many Asians do not know when they come to Britain that the British naming system is different from their own, or that the difference has any significance. They are likely to continue to use their names in the way they used them at home; for example, giving first names only (sometimes with a religious name) and omitting the family name (if there is one) even with officials and strangers.

As they become more familiar with British institutions they are likely to understand the importance of giving their names in a consistent way, and of using a family name in all records. Many people decide to adapt their own naming system to fit the British system. Unfortunately, people who seem to be changing their names are often met with suspicion, irritation or refusal.

East African Asians, who have a longer acquaintance with bureaucracy, are less likely to have trouble with their names in Britain. Many East African Asians, particularly men, will give their name in the form of initial(s) and surname. Some probing may be needed to get the first name(s) in full. Many Asian parents in Britain give their children only two names, which they use as a first name and surname, to fit the British system.

The spelling of Asian names in the Roman alphabet may vary a good deal since all Asian names are approximate transliterations from other alphabets. So members of the same family may each spell his/her name differently; for example, Choudrey, Chaudrey, Chaudhury, Chowdry or Choudhrey!

Talking with the family and friends

When talking with the family, or to people they know well, many Asians do not use first names. They use 'role' names such as 'brother', 'sister', 'uncle', 'aunt'. These role names do not necessarily indicate a family relationship. 'Brother', for example, may be used for a brother, a male relative of one's own generation, someone of the same age from one's village, or a close friend. This may cause confusion for British people when Asian people are introducing or talking about their families.

Because immigrant families are very often divided, it is not always useful for a health worker to find out the legal next-of-kin. It may be more useful to ask: Who is the most important person for us to speak to about you? I may need to speak to somebody in your family about you. Whom should I talk to?

Hindu names

The Hindu naming system (see Figure 4) is in three parts and slots very easily into the British system. Try to get all three names.

Figure 4 HINDU NAMING SYSTEM

	First name (personal, usually different male and female names)	Complementary name (different male and female names)	Subcaste name
female	Arima	Devi	Patel
male	Naresh	Lal	Chopra
	used by family and friends	used only with first name, *never* by itself	used like a British surname but indicates social status and traditional occupation; adopted by wife on marriage and shared by the whole family

Notes:

1 There are exceptions to the basic system shown here.

2 The complementary name may be used together with the first name, often as a mark of respect or on formal occasions.

3 When the first and complementary names are used together, they may be written as one word (Arimadevi) or as two (Arima Devi).

4 New complementary names may be adopted as one reaches adulthood or gets married.

5 The Hindu subcaste name most often heard in Britain is Patel, a Gujarati Hindu name.

Subcaste names

Some Hindus who disapprove of the caste system have dropped their last (subcaste) names, and may use their complementary names as surnames. For example, *Naresh Lal Chopra* may drop his subcaste name (Chopra) and become *Mr Lal.* But his daughter is not *Miss Lal*. Her full name is *Usha Devi Chopra*. If she drops her subcaste name she becomes *Miss Devi*. However, since the caste system is not so significant in Britain, people here may readopt their subcaste names and use them as surnames to fit the British system.

Sometimes, the record card of a Hindu patient may contain only the first and complementary names. This is usually not because the patient has chosen to drop the last (subcaste) name. It is the result of confusion when he first gave his name. It may be necessary to check this, and possibly to change the name on the record card, putting in the subcaste name as the patient's surname.

Gujarati Hindu names

Most Hindus in Britain come from Gujarati families. They sometimes have an additional name or names before the subcaste name. When they reach adulthood, men may use their father's first and complementary names after their own first and complementary names. For example, *Karam Chand Patel* adopts his father's names *Mohan Das,* and becomes *Karam Chand Mohan Das Patel.*

Women may use their father's first and complementary names before marriage and their husband's after marriage. For example, *Ushabehn Patel* is the daughter of *Somabhai Patel* and is called *Ushabehn Somabhai Patel.* She marries *Ravjibhai Patel* and becomes *Ushabehn Ravjibhai Patel.*

A list of Hindu names common in Britain will be found on page 100.

Sikh names

The Sikh naming system (see Figure 5) is based on the Hindu, but with several important differences. In the early days of Sikhism, all Sikhs were commanded to drop their subcaste names. All Sikh men adopted the name *Singh* as a complementary name, and all Sikh women adopted the name *Kaur*.

The subcaste name is rarely used by Sikhs in rural India, though most Sikhs in Britain now use it to fit the British system. How-

Figure 5   SIKH NAMING SYSTEM

First name (personal, usually the same male or female names)	Complementary/ religious name	Subcaste name
Jaswinder	(all females) Kaur	Gill
Armarjit	(all males) Singh	Samra
used by family and friends	used with the first name as a polite form of address	used like a British surname; adopted by the wife on marriage and shared by the whole family

Notes: 1   There are exceptions to the basic system shown here.

2   First names often end in -want, -inder, of -jit.

3   Some Sikhs will not use a subcaste name.

4   Singh and Kaur are not family names and are not used like British surnames. A Sikh man from the subcontinent may give his surname as **Singh**, but his wife will **not** be Mrs Singh, and his daughter will **not** be Miss Singh. They may, however, give their surnames as Mrs, or Miss, Kaur. Some East African Sikh families use **Singh** as a family name.

ever, devout Sikhs, particularly older women, may be most reluctant to give their subcaste names, and may consider it sinful. Except in these cases, try to get three names for Sikh patients.

Moslem names

Moslem names are generally the most difficult. *Traditionally, no name is shared by the whole family. Wives and children do not adopt the husband's name.* People may have two, three or more names, and it is not easy to fit them into the British naming system. Some Moslems try to fit their names to the British system and use a name common to the whole family. Other do not, and may find the system used for British records confusing, particularly if the names they give are then used wrongly by British staff.

This section outlines the basic pattern of Moslem names and gives suggestions on how they can be entered in British records. This involves imposing some elements of the British naming system on Moslems without causing them offence.

The following information applies only to Moslems from India, Pakistan and Bangladesh, *not* to Moslems from the Middle East or other areas.

Moslem men   usually have two or more names. One will be a personal name and one may be a religious title. The personal name, the equivalent of the British first name, *does not always come first.* It will usually follow a religious title. If a man does not have a religious title, the name he gives first is usually his personal name and can be entered as such.

Mohammed, the most common religious title, indicates that a man is a Moslem. It is *never* a personal or a 'first' name. (In Britain, due to misunderstandings, Mohammed has often been entered in records as the first name because it comes first. But calling a Moslem 'Mohammed' is like calling a Christian 'Christ' and can give great offence.) The personal name usually follows Mohammed: Mohammed *Arif,* Mohammed *Yusuf.* The personal name can be used alone, Yusuf, but is used with the religious title, Mohammed Yusuf, in more formal situations. So, when you enter Mohammed Yusuf's name in the record, put Mohammed in brackets to indicate that *Yusuf* is the personal name: (Mohammed) Yusuf. If Mohammed Yusuf has only these two names, enter *Yusuf* as his surname as well, so that his card can be correctly filed. Address him as *Mohammed Yusuf.*

Other names   Moslem families from urban areas are likely to use a family name or surname. This is, however, not done in the rural areas, from which most Moslems have come. Names other than personal names or religious titles are not usually surnames or family names in the British sense. They are usually given at birth, rather like a British middle name.

In some families each son will have a different name after his personal name. In others (especially in Britain), all the sons will have the same name. This may be a kind of clan or group name, possibly indicating traditional social status; for example, Chaudrey, Khan, Mia, Mieza, Qureishi, Rahman, Shah, Sheikh, Syed.

Here are some examples of male Moslem names with **personal** names in heavy (**bold**) type.

Aziz Rahman, Mohammed **Jabar** Mia, **Habibur** Rahman, Mohammed **Aziz**, Mohammed **Mansur** Chaudrey, **Yusif** Khan, **Shafiur** Hussein, **Monir** Uddin, Abdul **Rafiq**.

For British records, it is usually acceptable to use the final name as the surname even though this may also be the personal name.

Moslem women   in the subcontinent do not usually share a name with their husbands or children. When they first come to Britain,

Figure 6 ENTERING THE NAMES OF A MOSLEM FAMILY IN RECORDS

Family 1		
	Husband:	Mohammed Habibur Rahman
	Wife:	Jameela Kãtoon
	Son:	Shafiur Mia
	Daughter:	Shameema Bibi

Surname	*Other names*
RAHMAN	(Mohammed) Habibur
RAHMAN	Jameela Kãtoon w/o Mohammed Habibur *Rahman*
RAHMAN	Shafiur Mia s/o Mohammed Habibur *Rahman*
RAHMAN	Shameema Bibi d/o Mohammed Habibur *Rahman*

Family 2		
	Husband:	Khaliq Chaudry
	Wife:	Mahmuda Bibi
	Son:	Mohammed Hashim Chaudry
	Daughter:	Aziza Bibi

Surname	*Other names*
CHAUDRY	Khaliq
CHAUDRY	Mahmuda Bibi w/o Khaliq *Chaudry*
CHAUDRY	(Mohammed) Hashim s/o Khaliq *Chaudry*
CHAUDRY	Aziza Bibi d/o Khaliq *Chaudry*

Family 3		
	Husband:	Mohammed Arif
	Wife:	Razia Begum
	Son:	Amjad Iqbal
	Daughter:	Zeenat Bibi

Surname	*Other names*
ARIF	(Mohammed) Arif
ARIF	Razia Begum w/o Mohammed *Arif*
ARIF	Amjad Iqbal s/o Mohammed *Arif*
ARIF	Zeenat Bibi d/o Mohammed *Arif*

very few families know about the importance of records in our society, how they are organised, or that the records of the whole family are filed under a family surname. Many Moslem women find the idea of taking one of their husband's or father's names very odd. To them it means having a male name.

Most Moslem women from rural areas have two names: a personal name (Aziza, Fatma), and a title (Begum, Bibi, Kātoon, Kānoom, Nessa). The title is more or less equivalent to Miss or Mrs. It is *never* a surname. By convention, a woman is addressed informally by her personal name, and formally by her personal name and title; for example, Aziza Begum, Fatma Kātoon.

Entering Moslem names in British records   The British naming system can also be used for Moslem families, though it is important to realise that this will be strange to many Moslems and may be misunderstood at first.

It is nearly always acceptable to use the name of the male head of the household to identify the whole family. Use his *final* name as the surname for filing purposes. Indicate the relationship of other members to him with w/o (wife of), s/o (son of) or d/o (daughter of). Figure 6 shows how this can be done.

It is very important to remember that this is an imposed British adaptation of the Moslem naming system, for the purposes of records. It is NOT the patient's real name. Patients should still be addressed by their correct names. They will not respond unless the correct name, to which their ears are attuned, is used. For example, 'Mrs Rahman' and 'Mrs Chaudrey' will generally produce no response. When addressing or calling Moslem patients, use their own correct name (which they will be listening for) plus their (imposed) surname; for example, *Jameela Kātoon Rahman* and *Mahmuda Bibi Chaudrey*.

Gujarati Moslems who have often come to Britain via East Africa, usually *have* a family name. It is sometimes a Hindu name, and is used with a Moslem first name. For example, *Gulam Mohammed Patel, Jamal Ranji.*

Like a Gujarati Hindu, a Gujarati Moslem man may use his father's first name as a middle name. A woman before marriage may use her father's first name, or after marriage her husband's first name, as a middle name.

Registering a new patient

Remember that many patients from rural Asia will be unfamiliar with the kind of professional relationships that we are used to. Trust and cooperation are not generally given to people in authority unless some kind of personal relationship is felt. Any transaction is more likely to be successful if it is personalised. You may be pressed for time, but it is worth spending a little time to make sure that you get all the names a patient may have.

It is, of course, necessary, particularly where medical matters are concerned, to devise some system by which mistakes can be avoided. It must be borne in mind, however, that your Asian patient may be just as confused about giving his name as you are about recording it. Each patient's name may have to be worked out individually. When you ask a Moslem for a name, press for all the names you can get first, and fit them into the relevant slots on the form later.

Four general rules

1   If you think you are going to have difficulty, write the name down on a piece of paper first--then you can avoid spoiling the record card.

2   Get all the names you can, respecting the patient's possible scruples. For example, a devout Sikh woman may be reluctant to use her last name, and a Moslem woman may be reluctant to use her husband's name as a family name.

3   Sort out the full name so that it can be correctly written on a record card. Indicate any special features or usage in the name. If necessary, write a phonetic transcription beside the name for future guidance on correct pronunciation.

4   Passports and other documents from the patient's own country are not usually helpful because they reflect the usage of that country, which may be very flexible. They are neither a legal instruction nor a reliable guide on usage.

Listed below are some Hindu, Sikh and Moslem names which you are likely to come across, and this chapter ends with a practical exercise on names (Figure 7, pages 103–104).

Hindu names

Male personal names

Aditya	Damodar	Jaynati	Nirmal	Shanti
Ajay	Devendra	Jitendra	Prashant	Shiva
Amul	Dinesh	Kanti	Pritam	Subash
Anand	Ganesh	Kapil	Rajendra	Suman
Anil	Gopal	Karam	Rajesh	Sunil
Anoop	Govind	Kishore	Rakesh	Surendra
Arima	Gutam	Madav	Ram	Suresh
Arun	Haresh	Magan	Raman	Tarun
Atma	Jagil	Mani	Ramesh	Tushar
Bimal	Jayant	Naresh	Ravi	Vijay
Binoy	Jayesh	Niranjan	Satish	Virendra

Female personal names

Anurada	Hansa	Laxmi	Mukta	Saroj
Arima	Indira	Leela	Nirmala	Savita
Aroti	Jayashree	Leena	Nirupa	Shanta
Aruna	Jyoti	Lopa	Nivediua	Sharda
Bakula	Jyotsna	Madhavi	Pushpa	Shreeleka
Bimla	Kamla	Mani	Rama	Tara
Bindoo	Kanta	Manjula	Rohini	Tripta
Charulata	Krishna	Meena	Sadana	Usha
Ela	Lalita	Mira	Sandya	Vanita
Gayatri	Latika	Mohini	Saria	Vasundara

Subcaste names (common in Britain)

Advani	Choudhury	Hirani	Malhotra	Patel
Agarwal	Dasani	Iyer	Mashreuwala	Pradhan
Aiyar	Desai	Jain	Mehta	Rao
Amin	Desphande	Kazi	Mistry	Roy
Ashar	Dholakia	Kerai	Modi	Sethi
Badheka	Gaikwad	Kulkarni	Munshi	Shah
Bhanderia	Gohil	Kumar	Naidoo	Sharma
Chinoi	Gupta	Lad	Nayyar	Shenoy
Chopra	Halai	Lalwani	Patani	Vasani

Sikh names

Personal names

Ajit	Gurdas	Joginder	Piara
Amarjit	Gurmeet	Kamaljit	Pritam
Amrik	Gurwant	Kuldip	Rajinder
Amrit	Harbajan	Kulwant	Ramindar
Avtar	Harbans	Kushwant	Ranjit
Balbir	Harbinder	Malkiat	Ravinder
Balwinder	Hardip	Manjit	Sewan
Daljit	Inderjit	Mohan	Sohan
Davinder	Jaswant	Mohinder	Surjit
Dilbag	Jaswinder	Paramjeet	Swaran

Subcaste names (common in Britain)

Bains	Dhesi	Mann	Sahota
Bassi	Dhillon	Matharu	Sidhu
Bhumbra	Gill	Pannesar	Sohal
Birdi	Grewal	Rai	Sondhi
Brar	Johal	Randhawa	Takkar
Deol	Kalsi	Rayat	Uppal
Dhaliwal	Mangat	Samra	Virdi
Dhariwal	Manku	Sandhu	

Moslem names

Male personal names

Abbas	Farrukh	Latif	Rahman
Afzal	Ghafar	Mahmood	Rashid
Ahmed	Ghulam	Mahoud	Sadiq
Akbar	Gulab	Malik	Salim
Akram	Habib	Mansur	Samsur
Ali*	Hafeez	Massur	Shaif
Alam	Halim	Masud	Sharif
Amin	Hanif	Mia	Sulaiman
Amjad	Haq	Mir	Sultan
Anwar	Hasan	Miraj	Tariq
Araf	Hashim	Mubashir	Ubdaidullah
Arif	Hussein	Mukhtar	Uddin
Ashraf	Ibrahim	Muzzammil	Umar
Aslam	Ifthikhar	Nasim	Walid
Azam	Iqbal	Nasir	Yaqub
Aziz	Ishmael	Nurul	Yusaf
Badar	Ismael	Omar	Yusif
Badhur	Jafar	Osman	Yusuf
Badr	Jamal	Quasim	Zahid
Bashir	Kasem	Rafiq	Zubaida
Daud	Khaliq		

* Ali may also be a religious name, in which case it should never be used on its own.

Female personal names

Amina	Ismat	Nasreen	Sadaqat
Asia	Jameela	Parveen	Salma
Asmat	Kudeja	Rabia	Shamima
Ayesha	Kulsum	Razia	Sughra
Azara	Mahmuda	Razwana	Surriya
Aziza	Najma	Rokeya	Yasmin
Fatma	Naseema	Roushan	Zainab
Hamida	Nasrat	Sabera	

Figure 7 A PRACTICAL EXERCISE ON NAMES

How would you put these names on a record card? Can you identify the religion and sex of each person, and indicate where names are missing? Remember that for some Moslem patients you will need to ask some more questions about the personal or 'calling' name, and what name is used as a surname.

Answers on next page.

	First name	Other names	Surname	M/F	Religion
Mohammed Qamar Ahmed					
Tariq Abdul Aziz Ali					
Mohan Das					
Maganbhai Jayantilal Dasani					
Arima Devi					
Surjit Kaliba					
Jaswant Kaur					
Naresh Kumar					
Nasreem Akhtar Khan Noor					
Avtar Kaur Dhaliwal					
Jayendra Patel					
Amarjit Kaur Sandhu					
Amarjit Singh Sandhu					
Yaqub Shah					
Kulwant Singh Sangha					
Haresh Sharma					
Tripta Sharma					
Harbajan Singh					
Kasem Ali					
Syed Mohammed Maqsud Rahman					
Balbir Gill					

Figure 7   A PRACTICAL EXERCISE ON NAMES (Continued)

How did you get on?

A dash means that you don't have a name to put in that space.

A question mark means that you can't tell which name belongs in that space without asking the patient some more questions.

	First name	Other names	Surname	M/F	Religion
Mohammed Qamar Ahmed	?	Mohammed	?	M	Moslem
Tariq Abdul Aziz Ali	?	?	?	M	Moslem
Mohan Das	Mohan	Das	—	M	Hindu
Maganbhai Jayantilal Dasani	Maganbhai	Jayantilal	Dasani	M	Hindu
Arima Devi	Arima	Devi	—	F	Hindu
Surjit Kaliba	Surjit	—	Kaliba	?	Sikh
Jaswant Kaur	Jaswant	Kaur	—	F	Sikh
Naresh Kumar	Naresh	Kumar ?	Kumar ?	M	Hindu
Nasreem Akhtar Khan Noor	?	?	?	F	Moslem
Avtar Kaur Dhaliwal	Avtar	Kaur	Dhaliwal	F	Sikh
Jayendra Patel	Jayendra	—	Patel	M	Hindu
Amarjit Kaur Sandhu	Amarjit	Kaur	Sandhu	F	Sikh
Amarjit Singh Sandhu	Amarjit	Singh	Sandhu	M	Sikh
Yaqub Shah	Yaqub	—	Shah	M	Moslem
Kulwant Singh Sangha	Kulwant	Singh	Sangha	M	Sikh
Haresh Sharma	Haresh	—	Sharma	M	Hindu
Tripta Sharma	Tripta	—	Sharma	F	Hindu
Harbajan Singh	Harbajan	Singh	—	M	Sikh
Kasem Ali	?	?	?	M	Moslem
Syed Mohammed Maqsud Rahman	?	Mohammed	?	M	Moslem
Balbir Gill	Balbir	—	Gill	?	Sikh

Note to teachers and supervisors: this exercise may be reproduced if you wish to use it for teaching staff. Permission from the publishers is not required.

9 Personal hygiene

Personal cleanliness is linked with spiritual purity in Asian culture. People are accustomed to showering and changing their clothes two or three times a day. Members of all three major religions must prepare for prayer by washing. This is specifically prescribed in Islam. It is also most important to wash before eating.

Bathing and showering

People brought up in the Indian subcontinent generally prefer to wash standing up and in running water. Moslems and some members of other religious groups believe that water that has once been poured over the body should not touch it again.

Where there is no shower, people usually dip a bowl into a container, stand in the bath and pour water over themselves. This is considered much more hygienic than lying in a bath in the water one has washed in. Women after childbirth may be reluctant to lie down in hot salt baths.

Asian women are extremely modest, even in front of other women, and need complete privacy when they are washing or changing. Some women, particularly Moslems, never undress completely when bathing away from home; they may wear a petticoat or a towel while washing. In hospital, they will need a place to dry these after they have washed.

After bathing, both men and women may rub heavily scented oil into their bodies and hair to keep them soft and healthy. These oils may leave marks on bed linen.

Bathing the children

In their early days in Britain many Asians live in poor housing with either no bathrooms or with shared bathrooms which are very often cold and damp. They also worry that they or their children will catch a chill if they bath in cold weather. Some parents will need special advice about heating bathrooms safely, and dressing children up warmly after a bath. New mothers who are being taught to bath their babies may need very clear instructions about the temperature of the water and how to test it, and about drying the baby thoroughly.

Ritual washing

All Moslems are required to wash the face, from the elbows to the hands and from the knees to the feet before praying. Moslems may not pray if their bodies or clothes are dirty or soiled in any way. A Moslem patient in hospital, who is well enough to perform formal prayer, may ask for water for washing beforehand. He will require a bowl and a clean towel for this. Patients who cannot perform formal prayer are permitted to pray silently in bed. Even so, they may wish to wash first. Most Hindus and Sikhs also bath before formal prayer.

Care of the hair

The head is considered to be the most noble part of the human body. Ruffling a child's hair, or touching a Sikh's turban, may offend.

In a dusty tropical climate, the scalp tends to become dry and the hair brittle. People wash their hair very frequently and rub oil into it every day to protect it and keep it glossy. The massage is also believed to benefit the scalp. In Britain, this may be done only once a week and baby oil may be used. The oil may leave marks on a pillow.

Hair is an important part of a woman's beauty and traditionally is kept long. It is usually worn in a bun or in a long plait, which may be lengthened by adding an extra woollen plait. In conservative families, it is not considered proper for a girl or woman to let her hair hang loose. In less traditional families, particularly among East African Asians, young girls may cut their hair or wear it according to the current western fashion.

Some very traditional Hindu women will not wash their hair at the end of, or even during, pregnancy, or during menstruation.

Moslem women shave their pubic and underarm hair when they bath formally at the end of each menstrual period, and 40 days after giving birth.

The Sikh religion forbids the cutting or shaving of the hair, and most devout Sikhs will keep this rule. But many Sikh men in Britain have short hair and are clean-shaven. A Sikh man who has not cut his hair wears it tied on his head and fixed with a comb. He usually covers it with a turban. A new turban is usually made up and starched once a week. A Sikh boy whose parents do not wish him to cut his hair may wear it fixed on top of his head with a small white cloth (a rumāl).

If it is absolutely necessary for a Sikh patient to shave the head, the pubic region, or any other part of the body for a surgical operation, or before childbirth, careful explanation will be required to avoid extreme distress if the patient is a conservative Sikh.

Care of the teeth

Regular dental checkups are almost unknown in the rural subcontinent, and it is most unlikely that adults will attend a dentist regularly in Britain.

The teeth are traditionally cleaned by chewing on a special twig, the neem twig, which has cleansing properties. Neem twigs can be obtained in most of the larger Asian communities in Britain.

Some Asian children in Britain have bad teeth because of the greater availability of sweets, soft drinks and other harmful foods here. Parents may not realise that sweets are harmful. They will need advice about dental hygiene, and encouragement about regular visits to the dentist.

Cleaning the nose and mouth

Many Asians clear their nasal passages every morning by sniffing water up into the nose and blowing it out into a basin. The mouth is also rinsed. This is fairly noisy and may disturb British people who hear it, but most Asians do not feel clean and fit to start the day unless they have done it. They are generally unaware of the offence it gives to other people.

Lavatories

Most lavatories in Asia are of the squatting type, like many of those in Europe. This type is considered to be healthier and more hygienic than the seat type. Asians may find it repulsive to sit on a lavatory seat where other people have sat. They may squat on the seat instead. This may result in broken seats and dirty lavatories. However, most Asians in Britain become accustomed to sitting when using the lavatory.

Many Asians do not use lavatory paper but prefer to wash themselves, using their left hands. Though they may use lavatory paper, they often do not feel clean unless they have washed as well.

They may have to take some water into the lavatory to wash themselves with, since most lavatories in Britain do not have a source of running water. Water may be spilt on the floor, and unnecessary trouble can arise when the water is thought by other people to be urine. A source of running water in every lavatory cubicle would avoid this. The best solution may be to instal bidets.

Moslems are not allowed to pray if there is urine on their bodies or clothes. They must wash thoroughly after using the lavatory. This should also be remembered when a patient has to use a bedpan or bottle in hospital.

Touching or cleaning a lavatory may be considered ritually polluting as well as physically disgusting, particularly by Hindus. Members of the other religions, who have lived side by side with Hindus for centuries, may have adopted the same attitudes. If it is necessary to ask a patient to clean a lavatory after use, it is important to remember what this may mean to him or her.

Use of left and right hand

The left hand is generally used only for contact with the private parts. The right hand is used for all other purposes, including eating and picking things up. This custom has a religious force among Moslems. It must be borne in mind when organising things around a patient, particularly if the patient adheres to the custom very strictly. Food must be placed within reach of the right hand. Drips should, wherever possible, be put in the left arm. The locker should be placed on the right of the patient. Where a patient cannot, for some reason, use his or her right hand at all, extra care and help may be required.

Menstruation

This is considered embarrassing and disgusting and is rarely talked about. Menstrual blood is regarded as unclean and polluting, though the intensity of feeling about this and about childbirth bleeding will vary among individuals.

Some women carry on as normal when menstruating. Others—some Hindus and many Moslems—do not cook, and may remain isolated from the rest of the family at this time. Moslem women cannot fast when they are menstruating.

About three days after the menstrual bleeding stops, most women take a ritual bath to signal the end of the time of being unclean.* Until she has had the ritual bath, a Moslem woman cannot pray formally or touch the Koran.

In the subcontinent, most women use cotton cloths which are thrown away after use. East African Asian women, particularly

* See also Chapter 7, Mothers and babies, pages 73–86.

110

the younger ones, will be used to manufactured sanitary towels. In Britain, most Asian women soon learn to use these and married women may use tampons.

Since menstruation is a private, unmentionable subject, a woman in hospital or attending a clinic may try to dispose of a used sanitary towel or tampon down the lavatory, or even to hide it, rather than ask someone what to do. This can be extremely annoying to others and, in turn, extremely embarrassing to the Asian woman. When she comes into hospital, she may need to be shown how sanitary towels are disposed of.

10 Clothes, jewellery and makeup

Clothes

Immigrants tend to adopt the fabrics, if not the styles, of the clothes of the new country. They continue to wear what feels comfortable and correct. Clothes may have special significance as a way of retaining personal and cultural identity. The British, for example, lived and worked for decades in former colonies of the empire, but never adopted the dress of the local population. They felt it was important to maintain their own standards of dress and decency. The same is true of Asians in Britain.

Figure 8 WOMEN'S CLOTHES

	Pakistani Moslem	Punjabi Sikh	Gujarati Hindu	Gujarati Moslem	Bangladeshi Moslem
Women	shalwar (trousers)	shalwar (trousers)	blouse, sari and long	shalwar (trousers)	blouse, sari and long
	kameez (tunic)	kameez (tunic)	petticoat	kameez (tunic)	petticoat
	dupatta/ chadar (scarf)	dupatta/ chuni (scarf)		dupatta/ chuni (scarf)	(end of sari serves as veil)
Young girls	as above	as above	knee-length dress or trousers	as above	knee-length dress or trousers

113

Although some Asian women adopt western fashions, very many prefer to keep to their traditional styles. Most Asian men wear western-style street clothes, but they may wear traditional clothes at home to relax in. Older Gujarati men often wear white, and a white cap. Moslem men may wear a high-collared coat and a brimless hat.

Moslem women

Islamic law requires all Moslem women to keep their bodies, and the shape of their bodies, hidden.

Pakistani and Gujarati Moslem women wear shalwar (wide-leg trousers gathered slightly at the ankle and tied at the waist with a drawstring) and kameez (a long-sleeved tunic). The dupatta, chadar or chuni (a scarf) is worn so that it covers the bosom and can be pulled over the head, and sometimes across the face as a veil in the presence of strangers or guests unrelated to the family. Some Moslem women from Gujarat are less conservative in dress than women from Pakistan. Bangladeshi Moslem women usually wear a sari and use the end of it as a veil. Young Bangladeshi girls wear a knee-length dress or trousers until they reach puberty.

Punjabi Sikh women

Sikhs and Moslems lived side by side in the Punjab until 1949. Sikh women, like Moslem women, wear shalwar, kameez and dupatta, though the cut of these varies according to fashion. The dupatta should cover the bosom.

Both Sikh and Moslem women may wrap the dupatta around their heads when they are ill, as this is believed to ward off chills and infection.

Hindu women

Most Hindu women wear saris, sometimes with the midriff left bare. Traditionally, young Hindu girls wear a knee-length dress or blouse and skirt until puberty. After puberty, a girl should not show her legs. Older women and widows usually wear white, the colour of mourning.

East African Asian women

East African Asian women generally wear the clothes of the area from which their families originated. However, many professional East African women wear western clothes.

Clothes in hospital

Europeans have clothes for sleeping in and clothes for wearing out of bed. Asians are more likely to divide their clothes between those worn at home (in or out of bed) and those worn outside.

People may wear looser clothes at home. Men may wear pyjamas or a lungi (ankle-length cloth wrapped around the waist) around the house. Women wear the same kinds of clothes sleeping and waking. To find a woman sitting on her bed during the day in what may look like her nightclothes, or in bed in what look like her dayclothes, does not necessarily indicate that something is wrong.

Many women, British and Asian, buy nightclothes specially to come into hospital. Asian women should be advised to bring long nightdresses or petticoats, and long-sleeved bedjackets when coming to hospital, since they will wish to maintain standards of modesty while they are in bed, particularly in a public ward. A woman's legs must be covered right down to her ankles. If she has to put on a backless hospital gown, or to wear a hospital nightdress, she will need an ankle length petticoat to remain decent. She may also wish to keep her arms covered.

Dressing for the British climate

We can get several changes of weather in one day in Britain, and this presents many problems for Asians who are used to a constant, predictable climate.

They are accustomed to cotton, silk and nylon, but they may not know about other fabrics more suitable for the British climate. Most cold weather clothes need brushing and dry-cleaning: washing may ruin them. Asian women are used to putting on freshly washed clothes every day. In Britain, washing and drying clothes present new difficulties.

Many Asians, especially women, have never worn shoes which cover the feet entirely. They find such shoes uncomfortable and cramping, and many prefer to wear open-toe sandals, even in cold weather.

Practical advice may be needed on shopping, particularly for clothes and shoes for children, and on dressing for comfort throughout the day. Parents may find it difficult to select shoes for their children, getting the right sizes and fittings. They may send their children off to school on a bright morning without coats or waterproofs which they may need during the day.

Jewellery

Some items of jewellery have important religious significance, like the wedding ring of a European woman, and should never be removed. If it is essential to remove such an item, it is most important to make sure that the patient understands why, and that the jewellery will be kept safe and will be returned as soon as possible.

Some patients will be more concerned than others about this matter, but a patient who is already feeling vulnerable is likely to become the more upset if an important piece of religious jewellery is removed. It may even have been put on specifically to protect the patient during illness. Parents may be very distressed if they have put a religious article on a sick child and it has been removed without their consent.

Hindus

Wedding bangles   A Hindu woman puts on glass bangles at her wedding. They are not removed unless the husband dies, when the widow ceremonially shatters her wedding bangles. Breaking or removing wedding bangles is considered an extremely bad omen and will upset a Hindu woman as much as the loss or removal of a wedding ring would upset a European woman. It is often impossible to remove wedding bangles without breaking them.

Threads and necklaces   Some Hindus wear a thread round their bodies. It is put on at an important religious ceremony and should never be removed. Men of one Hindu sect, Swami Narayan, may wear a bead necklace.

Sikhs

Kara   This bangle, one of the five signs of Sikhism, is worn by men and women. It is never removed, even on death.

Kirpan   The dagger, another of the five signs, which all Sikhs, men and women wear, symbolises their warrior brotherhood.

In Britain, except on formal religious occasions, most Sikhs carry a symbolic dagger or wear a dagger-shaped brooch or pendant. Some hospital authorities have mistaken a symbolic dagger for a dangerous weapon.

Wedding bangles   Some Sikh women wear glass wedding bangles, and these may have the same significance as Hindu wedding bangles.

Moslems

Religious protection   Many Moslems, particularly Pakistanis, wear a stone or medallion on a string round the neck, arm or waist. It may be engraved with a short prayer or a verse of the Koran. Moslems may also wear a very small leather or cloth bag or metal container on a string which also generally contain verses of the Koran. These items are to protect them and to give strength during childbirth or a surgical operation. Patients often put them on specially before coming into hospital, and will become most distressed if they are removed.

Nose jewels   Instead of wedding bangles, Bangladeshi women sometimes wear a jewel in the nose. This is as important as the wedding bangles and should not be removed unless absolutely necessary.

Other jewellery

Asian women also wear earrings, decorative bangles and rings (sometimes wedding rings). A child may wear jewellery given by relatives, often in celebration of its birth. A lot of this jewellery is extremely precious. People who cannot understand the assurances of hospital staff may be very worried that their jewellery will be lost or stolen if it is removed.

Makeup

Certain kinds of makeup are traditional. Western-style makeup is usually disapproved of. It is not worn in rural India, though Asian women from East Africa may wear it.

Bindi (or tika) is a coloured spot worn on the forehead by Hindu and some Sikh women. It indicates that a married woman has performed her morning prayer, though it may nowadays be worn purely as decoration. Widows do not wear it.

Both men and women of the Hindu sect, Swami Narayan, may wear a red spot on the forehead.

Hair parting Traditional Hindu wives, especially when they are newly married, paint a red streak into their hair partings. This is less common in Britain.

Surma (surana or kajil) is black eye makeup worn in the Indian subcontinent and the Middle East. It is put around the eyes and inside the eyelids and is believed to have cooling and antiseptic properties. Some varieties have been found to contain lead sulphide and their importation to Britain has been banned. It is important to try to persuade families to use an anti-allergic mascara instead of surma, and to explain the dangers of using *any* product which does not list its ingredients.

Traditional mothers may also put a black spot on the temple or cheek of a baby to protect it from harm.

Henna (or mandi) paste may be painted on the hands for special occasions such as weddings. The colour may remain on the skin for several days.

11 Food

Religious restrictions

Religious restrictions about food are part of the Asian way of life, and in rural areas of the subcontinent very few people would consider breaking them. Most people feel physical revulsion at the thought. If they have broken them, even unknowingly, they feel sick, disgusted and guilty. As they come into contact with British

Figure 9 A SHORT LIST OF PERMITTED AND PROHIBITED FOODS

	Hindus	*Sikhs*	*Moslems*
Eggs	some*	yes	yes
Milk and yoghurt	yes	yes	yes
Cottage/curd cheese	yes	yes	yes
Chicken	no	some	halal†
Mutton	no	some	halal†
Beef	no	no	halal†
Pork	no	rarely	no
Fish	no	some	yes
Butter/ghee	yes	yes	yes
Other animal fats (lard)	no	some	halal†

* Very strict Hindus do not eat eggs.

† Halal meat must be killed in a special way (see page 123).

Note: This table gives only general information. Individual Asians will vary in the extent to which they adhere to these rules.

121

society, some Asians, particularly men, may relax some of the restrictions, though they are likely to keep to the really important ones. For example, a Moslem would not eat pork, and most Sikhs and Hindus would not eat beef. But there are now many Asians in Britain, especially children brought up here, who eat an entirely western diet. It is usually the women, of all three religious groups, who adhere most faithfully to food restrictions.

Hindu restrictions

Hindus believe in the interdependence of all life, and will not eat any food that has involved the taking of life. Some Hindus will not eat eggs, since they are potentially a source of life. Hindus rely for their protein on dairy products and pulses such as lentils, split peas and beans. Some Hindus do not eat onions or garlic. Yoghurt and home-made curd cheese are important in the diet. Western cheese is not suitable for strict vegetarians because it is made with animal rennet. Most Asians dislike western cheese anyway.

Most Gujarati Hindus are strict vegetarians. Some East African Gujarati Hindus may be less strict, but this depends largely on the community they come from and cannot be assumed.

Beef and other meat   The cow is a sacred animal. The slaughter of cows has been forbidden in India since the seventh century. Even Hindus who are not strict vegetarians will generally not eat beef. Some Hindus will eat other kinds of meat, but not pork which is considered unclean. They may also eat white (non-oily) fish.

Fasting   In addition to certain fast days in the religious calendar, may devout Hindus fast regularly on one or two days a week (often Tuesdays and Fridays), or on the day of a new moon. Some people abstain from all food; others eat only foods that are considered pure, such as fruit, yoghurt, nuts or potatoes.

Cooking   Some devout Hindus will only eat food prepared by a member of the same caste. In a few cases, this may be a reason why a Hindu patient refuses all food in hospital.

Sikh restrictions

Beef and other meat   Most Sikhs eat meat, though some are vegetarians. Very few Sikhs eat beef, and they may not eat pork because it is considered unclean. A few Sikhs do not eat eggs.

Fasting   Some very devout Sikhs fast in the same way as Hindus. They may fast on certain days.

Moslem restrictions

Islam lays down precise laws about what can and cannot be eaten, and how food should be prepared. Most Moslems, whether from the Indian subcontinent or from East Africa, are traditional in their eating habits.

Pork   Moslems are expressly forbidden to eat pork or anything made with pork. Great care is generally taken not to break this prohibition. Some Moslems will not eat commercial bread, cakes, biscuits or jellies in case they contain pork products.

Other meat   Moslems can eat all other meat provided that it is 'halal', that is, killed in the prescribed way. The animal must bleed to death, and must be dedicated to God by a Moslem. All animal products used in food preparation must be halal. For this reason, although they are not vegetarian, most Moslems will not eat meat or other dishes away from home, or buy proprietary baby foods, since they may contain non-halal meat products.

Fish   Fish is considered to have died naturally when taken out of the water. The question of halal, therefore, does not arise. But Moslems cannot eat fish that does not have fins or scales. Asian Moslems are unfamiliar with most kinds of fish found in Britain and may not know which are permitted. They may not buy tinned or prepared fish.

Fasting   During the month of Ramazan, Moslems must abstain from all food, all liquid, and tobacco, between dawn (one and a half hours before sunrise) and sunset. Children under 12, and old people, are exempted. People who are ill or on a journey, and women who are menstruating, pregnant, or breast feeding, should not fast during Ramazan, but must make a compensatory fast at some other time. Although sick people are exempted, very devout Moslems may wish to fast, and this may include not taking medicines by mouth. Special provision may be required in hospital for Moslem patients who wish to fast.

During Ramazan most Moslem families get up an hour or two before dawn and eat a good breakfast before the fast begins. After sunset, they have another fairly large meal. Many people experience faintness and lethargy during the long day without food or drink.

Asian food in Britain

Asian housewives continue as far as possible to cook what they cooked at home. This is what they know, and what they and their families like. The food in the different areas from which Asians have come varies according to local climate, local agricultural produce and the religion of the people.

Meals

Most families eat three meals a day. In Britain, breakfast usually consists of tea (made by boiling the tea, water, milk, sugar and sometimes spices, all together), cereal with milk and sugar, an egg with bread and butter, or rice or chapatis with yoghurt or butter-milk.

Lunch and dinner consist of a staple starch (chapatis or rice), two or three main dishes (pulses and a vegetable or meat curry), often with fruit and yoghurt or a home-made pudding of semolina. A housewife on her own will probably eat only a light lunch.

It is important to remember, when advising about diet, that even non-vegetarian Asians usually eat meat in very small quantities, often with a lot of sauce. As a matter of etiquette, some women give all the meat to their husbands and children. Even non-vegetarians, therefore, particularly women, may be taking only very small quantities of animal protein.

Some main food items

Chapatis   flat, unleavened pancakes made of wheat flour and water. The flour is 85 per cent wholemeal. Most chapati flour sold in this country—like the flour used for British bread—is fortified with iron, calcium and certain B vitamins. An adult may eat six to eight chapatis a day.

Curd cheese   People from the Indian Punjab often make and eat a lot of curd cheese (paneer). Manufactured curd and cottage cheeses are mild in flavour and suitable for vegetarians. It may be useful to encourage the use of these in cooking.

Ghee   butter boiled for about an hour to clarify it and reduce the moisture content—the great advantage is that it does not burn easily.

Figure 10 REGIONAL DIETS OF THE MAIN ASIAN GROUPS IN BRITAIN

| | From the INDIAN PUNJAB | | From GUJARAT | | From PAKISTAN | From BANGLADESH |
	SIKHS	HINDUS	HINDUS	MOSLEMS	MOSLEMS	MOSLEMS
Staple starch	chapatis	chapatis	chapatis rice	chapatis or rice	chapatis	rice
Cooking oil	ghee	ghee	groundnut oil (some ghee)	groundnut oil (some ghee)	ghee/ groundnut oil	groundnut oil (some ghee)
Meat	no beef some are vegetarians others eat some meat (mainly chicken and mutton; no pork)	no beef mostly vegetarians	no beef mostly vegetarians	no pork or pork products halal meat only (usually chicken or mutton)	no pork or pork products halal meat only (usually chicken or mutton)	no pork or pork products halal meat only (usually chicken or mutton) fresh or dried fish
Eggs	not a major part of the diet	not eaten by strict vegetarians	not eaten by strict vegetarians	usually hard-boiled or fried	usually hard-boiled or fried	usually hard-boiled or fried

	very important:	very important:	important, especially	fairly important	fairly important:	few or none
Dairy products	yoghurt buttermilk home-made cream cheese milk (boiled, sweetened)	yoghurt buttermilk home-made cream cheese milk (boiled, sweetened)	milk (boiled, sweetened) and yoghurt		yoghurt milk (boiled, sweetened)	
Pulses	a major source of protein	may be almost the only source of protein	may be almost the only source of protein	fairly important	few pulses some dahl	few pulses some dahl
Vegetables	vegetable curries occasional salad fresh fruit	vegetable curries occasional salad fresh fruit	vegetable curries occasional salad fresh fruit	vegetable curries occasional salad fresh fruit	vegetable curries occasional salad fresh fruit	vegetable curries salads (undressed) fresh fruit

Jaggery   unrefined brown sugar containing iron.

Pulses, dahls and grams   Pulses are the seeds of leguminous vege-tables, high in vegetable protein. There are over 60 varieties, such as bengal gram, black gram, green gram and chickpeas. The whole seed is called a 'gram'. The split seed is a 'dahl'. Pulses can also be used as a flour (besan). Pulses usually need a very long preparation time.

Shopping and cooking

Asian housewives, like those of other minority groups, may run into problems when shopping and cooking for their families. There are Asian shops in most areas where most Asian house-wives shop, but most imported foods are very expensive and are neither as nutritious nor as tasty as fresh food. Families often spend a disproportionate amount of their income on food.

Many Asian housewives would welcome information and practical advice on how to buy and cook British fruit and vegetables which are fresh, cheaper, and can usually be prepared so that the flavour is acceptable to Asian tastes.

Children's food

Asian children, particularly Hindus and Moslems, may obey religious restrictions about food at school. This will depend mainly on the orthodoxy of their parents.

Some Asian children eat little or nothing in the middle of the day, either because the food offered at school is not permitted (the vegetarian alternative may contain eggs, or cheese, or it may have come into contact with prohibited food), or because the only permitted food offered—potatoes and boiled vegetables—is boring and unappetising. This is particularly serious for vegetarian children, who need a good helping of food containing protein three times a day.

The children often pick up the less desirable eating habits of other British children. They eat icecream, sweets, soft drinks, crisps and chips, which contain little other than calories. Again this is particularly serious for vegetarian children. Many children introduce these into their homes. Some mothers cook 'convenience food' such as fish fingers and baked beans for their children, though they probably do not like them themselves. Some children refuse to eat anything else, or to touch their parents' food.

Special beliefs and customs

Hot and cold foods

Certain foods are believed to have a heating or cooling effect upon the body, the emotions and the personality. This has nothing to do with the temperature of the food. Food that is salty, acid, or high in animal protein is generally considered 'hot'. Food that is sweet, bitter, or astringent in flavour is generally considered 'cold'. 'Hot' foods are believed to cause over-excitement, giddiness, inflammatory reactions, sweating and fatigue. 'Cold' foods are believed to cool the body and to give strength, calm, and cheerfulness.

The following is a list of foods that, according to the Hindu tradition, have 'hot' or 'cold' properties. In Moslem traditions, some of these foods may have different qualities.

Hot   lentils, carrots, onions, eggplant, chilli, ginger, dates, eggs, meat, fish, tea, honey, brown sugar.

Cold cereals, green gram (moong), chickpeas, red gram (toor), all green leafy vegetables, potatoes, most other vegetables, all nuts, most fruits (including apple, orange, banana, lemon), milk and dairy products, white sugar.

Most people pay little attention to these beliefs in their everyday lives, and diets are usually balanced, though housewives may prepare more 'cold' food in the summer and more 'hot' food during the winter. These beliefs generally only become important when someone is ill, or when a woman is pregnant or breast feeding.

Diet during pregnancy

Pregnant women traditionally avoid certain foods. Practices vary a good deal and it is impossible to say for certain who will or will not eat what.

Pregnancy is considered to be a 'hot' condition so 'hot' foods are avoided. It is believed that 'hot' foods in early pregnancy may cause a miscarriage. Most pulses are 'hot', but green gram is considered 'cold' and so can be recommended when a woman needs extra protein. Meat is 'hot' and even a non-vegetarian woman may avoid it while she is pregnant.

Gujaratis and Punjabi Sikh women drink a lot of milk when they are pregnant. Some women may fast during the last month or so of pregnancy in order to keep the weight of the baby down, and so make the birth easier.

Immediately after the birth, a mother is given special delicacies which are believed to promote lactation. One such dish, 'dhabra', is made from almonds, butter, sugar and cream. Certain other dishes are considered extremely nourishing and women after childbirth should eat a little of them every day. Moslem women often drink a thick rich broth. Lentils and other 'hot' foods are also believed to increase the milk supply. Certain foods, such as oranges or grapes, are not allowed as they are believed to give the baby loose stools. Some women eat 'hot' foods immediately after giving birth as they are believed to have a purgative and cleansing effect. It is believed that if a woman eats 'cold' foods while she is breast feeding, she may give her child a cold.

Diet during illness

Sick people eat soft foods, with few if any spices. People from different areas will have different food preferences: Indian Punjabis might eat thick soups and more dairy products to make them well; Gujaratis are more likely to eat thin lentil soups, 'kitcheree' (rice and green gram), nuts, or sweets made with nuts.

An adult with a cold or a cough may avoid 'cold' foods, but if he is feverish he may eat 'cold' foods to bring the temperature down.

Eating in hospital

For many Asian patients this is a major problem. Many foods are forbidden by their religion. The food offered may be unfamiliar, and patients will often refuse it in case it contains any forbidden ingredients.

Hospital food may be their first encounter with British food. Most people find a strange diet even less appetising when they are ill; they crave familiar food. Eating in hospital, therefore, can cause real anxiety and distress. It may be the reason why Asian patients discharge themselves from hospital.

Food brought by the family

The families of many Asian patients try to solve the problem by bringing food in as often as they can, though they may not be able to come often enough. Bringing food is standard practice in most rural hospitals in the subcontinent. The patients' families are largely responsible for feeding and looking after them. Female relatives usually bring food from home, or cook it in the hospital. In some British hospitals, it is quite acceptable for visitors to bring food to patients; in others it arouses irritation, and this adds to the patients' feelings of isolation and unease.

If a hospital is not able to provide adequate and palatable food for Asian patients, staff may wish to consider encouraging the families to bring food in. Families may need advice on what to bring. Light and nourishing dishes, such as yoghurt, vegetables, soups, meat or vegetable curry with few spices, are usually suitable.

It will also be necessary to make certain arrangements in the ward. Patients must be able to wash their hands before and after eating. Some, particularly Moslems, must also rinse their mouths with clean water after eating.

Patients may also need their own plates and other utensils, and facilities for washing up and for heating and storing food. Privacy may be required while eating. It must be remembered that in Asian culture only the right hand should be used for picking up food. This has religious force for Moslems. Make sure, therefore, that a patient can always reach his food with the right hand.

*Choosing suitable food from the hospital menu**

Unless a hospital is serving Asian food, very little that is on the menu will be suitable. Some Asian patients may want to eat the food provided and will need some help in choosing dishes which will not conflict with religious beliefs. Three main points must be borne in mind.

1 *Food which contains any forbidden ingredients at all is forbidden.* For example, eggs fried in bacon fat, and puddings cooked in cake tins greased with lard, are forbidden to Moslems and to vegetarian Hindus and Sikhs.

2 *Food which has been in contact with forbidden food is forbidden.* A vegetarian Hindu cannot eat salad on a plate that contains, or has once contained, a piece of meat or any meat product such as gravy, since the whole dish is then contaminated. A vegetarian cannot eat potatoes or cabbage with meat gravy. A Moslem cannot eat from a dish that has contained non-halal meat.

3 *Strict vegetarians need at least one serving of vegetable protein at each meal to obtain sufficient protein.* To ensure this, the hospital should offer at least one acceptably flavoured dish of pulses (lentils, chickpeas, split peas, grams) at each meal, in addition to other suitable food.

In addition, three other points should be remembered.

1 The 'curries' served in British hospitals do not usually resemble Asian food, and most Asian patients find them as unappetising as much other British food.

---

* For people who would like more specific guidance on the preparation of food for Asian patients in hospital, the DHSS Catering and Dietetic Branch has in press a handbook, *Catering for minority groups,* for use by NHS caterers, dietitians and nurses.[16]

2   The texture of short grain (pudding) rice is not suitable for main course meals.

3   Vegetarians rely heavily on milk as a nutritional source. They may wish to drink several pints of milk a day while they are in hospital. Many Asians, both adult and children, like their milk boiled and sweetened.

Medically specified or restricted diets

Where a check is being kept on the patient's intake, it is important to explain (using an interpreter if necessary) exactly what is required and why. The idea of keeping precise records or sticking to a scientifically worked-out diet may not be understood or accepted. In cases where special diets, such as low fat or high roughage, are required it is also important to explain everything clearly to the patient's family.

Good examples of some special diets suitable for Asian patients can be obtained from the community dietitian of the Greater Glasgow Health Board.* The sample diets have been worked out to cover anaemia, heartburn, morning sickness, low salt content, constipation, weight reduction and pregnancy, taking religious restrictions into account.

An overweight British patient might be told to cut out rice, pasta, jams, cakes, sweets and biscuits altogether, cut down on bread and potatoes, and not spread too much butter on his bread. For an Asian patient, little of this would be relevant. He is unlikely to eat cakes, biscuits or buttered bread anyway. He would probably eat sweets only at very special celebrations. On the other hand, most curries contain a lot of butter, ghee or oil: it is almost impossible

* Ingram Street, Glasgow G1 1ET. Enclose a large stamped addressed envelope with your enquiry.

to make a curry without fat. An Asian patient might find it difficult to cut out rice or chapatis altogether since these are an intrinsic part of each meal, and not an optional extra. He could, however, be advised to avoid fried foods such as puris and paratas (types of fried pancake).

Dietary advice must be given in accordance with the religious beliefs of the patient and should be based on his normal food habits. This is the only advice likely to be successful. Get to know what people are used to eating. Every diet contains a preferred source of protein and other nutrients. Find out what these are for each patient and mention them in your advice.

Traditional beliefs about food may conflict with your advice. The patient may not volunteer this information, particularly if he feels that you will disapprove. It is therefore wise to ask whether he will be able to follow your advice.

Recent research

A study of the diets of Ugandan Asian refugees in the UK showed that almost all the families studied were below the DHSS-recommended intakes of energy, iron, protein and, particularly, vitamin D.[8] Deficiencies were more serious among Hindu families.

The survey found that many families felt lethargic and did not know which foods to buy to supplement their diets. People may attribute their lethargy to other causes, such as a change of climate or of daily routine.

Hindus and vegetarian Sikhs are therefore especially likely to be at risk nutritionally.

Nutritional requirements and acceptable sources

Iron from vegetable sources is badly absorbed and almost all vegetarians, particularly women, are likely to suffer from iron deficiency. Citrus fruits or juices, eaten at the same time, help the absorption of iron.

Sources of iron acceptable in a vegetarian diet

almonds	* dark green leafy	jaggery (unrefined
broccoli	vegetables (mustard	brown sugar)
butterbeans	leaves, spinach,	leeks
carrots (canned)	watercress, cabbage)	lentils
chapati flour	* dried fruit	Marmite
cocoa powder	† egg yolk	millet
	* haricot beans	* peas
		* pulses
		treacle

* Very good source.
† Not suitable for strict vegetarians.

Vitamin B_{12} and folic acid deficiencies are common among Asians. Failure to conceive may be caused by a diet deficient in vitamin B_{12}. Vegetarian Asians may not be able to eat most of the foods available in Britain that contain vitamin B_{12} and may have to take tablets to remedy the deficiency. Milk and milk products contain vitamin B_{12}, but boiling the milk may destroy the vitamin, and many Asians drink their milk boiled and sweetened.

Sources of vitamin B₁₂

buttermilk	* herrings
* cheese (hard)	Marmite
dried milk	* sardines
† eggs	

* Not suitable for vegetarians.

† Not suitable for strict vegetarians.

Folic acid can be completely lost in cooking. Imported and stored vegetables usually lose their folic acid. Extra folic acid is required by anybody, especially a pregnant woman, suffering from thalassaemia.

Sources of folic acid acceptable in a vegetarian diet

beetroot	dried figs	parsnips
broccoli	* egg yolk	peas
brussels sprouts	grams	spinach
cabbage	kidney beans	watercress
cauliflower	nuts	wholemeal bread
dates	parsley	wholemeal flour

* Not suitable for strict vegetarians.

Vitamin D   deficiency is a serious problem among Asians in Britain and is chiefly found in young children, adolescents, and pregnant and lactating women. A vegetarian diet and lack of exposure to sunlight may be significant causes.

Many girls and women spend most of their time indoors, and cover their bodies completely, so there is very little exposure to sunlight. Asian mothers may be afraid to take their children out in the cold British weather. When they *do* take them out they wrap them up so well that no sunlight gets to any part of them.

Sources of vitamin D

for non-vegetarians	for vegetarians
egg yolk	butter
fish oils	cream cheese
hard cheese	* egg yolk
herrings	margarine
mackerel	milk (evaporated and whole dried)
sardines	yoghurt (if fortified)

* Not suitable for strict vegetarians.

Margarine, which is often fortified with vitamin D, is not widely used by Asians because it is unfamiliar and people are not sure whether it contains forbidden ingredients. In recommending margarine, it is important to tell people which brands of fortified margarine contain *only* vegetable oils and to stress that the vitamin itself is not from an animal. For those people who usually cook with ghee and like a buttery flavour, it may be possible to recommend the use of ghee made with half margarine and half butter. Ghee made in this way also stays soft in cold weather.

For people who make their own yoghurt at home, it might be useful to recommend adding dried milk powder to the milk beforehand, or making yoghurt from evaporated milk. Certain commercial brands of yoghurt are also fortified and this is marked on the container.

Most fish is acceptable to non-vegetarians, but it is unfamiliar to people from land areas of Indian and Pakistan and so is not usually included in their diet. Bangladeshis, on the other hand, usually include a lot of fish in their diet.

Protein deficiency usually goes with calorie deficiency and in Britain is, therefore, usually found in people who are not eating enough. This may be because they cannot buy familiar foods or because food is too expensive. Some people suffering from depression may not be eating enough. Protein deficiency is also found in infants who are fed over-diluted foods.

Sources of protein acceptable in a vegetarian diet

broad beans	pulses (see page 135)
chapati flour	rice
dairy products	semolina
* eggs	soya flour
millet	vermicelli
† nuts	

* Not suitable for strict vegetarians.

† Unlikely to be eaten in large quantities.

Foods in English and Hindi–Urdu

Although only the Hindi–Urdu phonetic translation is given here, many of these names are common throughout Northern India. There are, however, some regional or local variations in the names and in pronunciation. Some foods do not exist in the subcontinent and, therefore, have no Hindi–Urdu names.

MEAT:	MEAT/GOSHT:
FISH	MACHLĪ/MACHĪ
Chicken	Murghī/Murghā
Duck	Batakh
Fish	Machlī/Machī
Goat	Bakrā/Bakrī
Kidney	Gurdā
Liver	Kalēji
Meat	Gosht/Meat

139

| MEAT: | MEAT/GOSHT: |
| FISH (continued) | MACHLĪ/MACHĪ (continued) |

Minced meat	Keema
Mutton/Lamb	Bakreka gosht
Prawns	Jheenga
Rabbit	Khargōsh

| VEGETABLES | SABZJI/BHĀJI |

Beans (baked)	Baked beans
Beans (broad)	Fārma fali
Beans (green)	Hari sāim
Beans (haricot)	Sāim ki fali
Cabbage	Band gobī
Carrot	Gājar
Cauliflower	Ful gobī
Coriander leaves	Hara dhania
Cucumber	Kheera
Eggplant (aubergine)	Baingan/Batāūn
Gourd (bitter)	Karēla
Ladies' fingers (okra)	Bhindi
Lettuce	Salād/Bata
Mushrooms	Khumb
Mustard leaves	Saag/Sarson Ka Saag
Onion	Payāz
Pea	Mutter
Pepper (green)	Simla mirich
Potato	Aloo
Pumpkin	Petāh
Spinach	Pālak
Squash	Kadoo/Ghia
Sweet potato	Shākarkūndi
Tomato	Tamāter
Turnip	Shalgam

PULSES   DHAL

There are about 20 different kinds of pulses or grams in common use in the Indian subcontinent, many of which are available in Britain. Not all of these have an English name.

Black gram	Urad
Chickpeas	Kabuli chanā
Green gram	Moong
Kidney beans	Rajma/Motī
Lentil	Masoor
Red gram	Toor
Split peas	Chanē ki dhal

There are other kinds of pulses with no English equivalent, such as *Arhar* and *Miti*.

Dhal means washed and split pulses (often yellow, whatever their original colour): *urad dhal, moong dhal, masoor ki dhal, chanē ki dhal.*

Sābut means unsplit pulses in the skin: *sābut moong* which has a green skin, and *sābut urad* which has a black skin.

CEREALS   ANĀJ

Arrowroot	Arahōt
Barley	Jaū
Bread (loaf)	Double Roti
Corn (maize)	Makaī
Cornflour	Makaī ka ata
Flour	Ata
Flour (gram)	Bēsan
Flour (white)	Meda
Millet	Bājra
Oatmeal porridge	Dalīa

CEREALS (continued) ANĀJ (continued)

Rice	Chāwal
Sago	Sabudāna
Semolina	Sūji
Vermicelli	Sēvian

FRUIT FAL

Apple	Seb
Banana	Kelā
Currant	Munāka
Date	Khajoor
Fig	Anjeer
Grape	Anjoor
Grapefruit	Grapefruit/Chakotra
Lemon	Bara nĩmbu
Lime	Nĩmbu
Lychee	Lichĩ
Mango	Aam
Mango juice	Aam ka ras
Melon (sweetmelon)	Kharbooza
Melon (watermelon)	Tarbooz
Orange	Mālta
Orange juice	Mālte ka ras
Peach	Arōō
Pear	Nāshpati
Pineapple	Ananas
Plum	Aloobokhāra
Prune	Sūkha aloobokhāra
Raisin	Kishmish
Sultana	Kishmish
Tangerine	Santra

NUTS	MĒWA
Almond	Badaam
Cashew	Kajū
Coconut	Narial
Dried coconut	Kōpra/Kopa
Peanut	Moong fali
Pinenut	Chilgōza
Pistachio	Pista
Walnut	Akhrōt

MILK, MILK PRODUCTS	DOODH
Butter	Mākhan
Butter (clarified)	Ghee
Cheese	Paneer
Cheese (curd)	Paneer
Clotted cream	Malāi
Dried milk	Sūkha doodh
Eggs	Andā
Egg white	Andē ka sufēd
Egg yolk	Andē ki zārdi
Egg (boiled)	Ublā andā
Egg (fried)	Tala anda
Milk	Doodh
Yoghurt	Dahi

SPICES, HERBS AND CONDIMENTS	MASĀLA
Bay leaf	Tēz pattāh
Cardamon (big)	Bari elāchi
Cardamon (white)	Chhōti elāchi
Caraway	Kalā zeera

143

SPICES, HERBS AND
CONDIMENTS (continued)   MASALA (continued)

Chillies (green)	Hari mirich
Chillies (red)	Lāl mirich
Cinnamon	Dalchīni
Clove	Laung
Coriander	Dhania
Cumin	Sufēd zeera
Garlic	Lassan
Ginger	Adrāk
Mixed spice	Garam masāla
Mustard seed	Raī
Pepper (black)	Kāli mirich
Peppercorns	Sābut kāli mirich
Pickle	Achār
Salt	Nimāk/Namāk
Turmeric	Haldi

IMPLEMENTS/CONTAINERS

Fork	Kanta
Knife	Churī/Chakū
Spoon	Chanmāch
Big spoon	Bara chanmāch
Small spoon	Chota chanmāch
Bottle	Bōtel
Small bottle	Shishi
Tin	Teen
Tinned	Teen me
Packet (small box-shaped)	Dibbi
(large box-shaped)	Dibba
(in wrapper)	Paket

MISCELLANEOUS

Baking powder	Pakānē ka sodā
Biscuit	Biscoot
Cake	Cake
Honey	Shēhad
Juice	Ras
Oil	Tale
Fish oil	Machī ka tale
Groundnut oil	Moongfalī ka tale
Olive oil	Zaitūn ka tale
Rosewater	Gulāb ka ark
Silver leaves	Chāndi ka wark
Sugar (unrefined brown)	Jaggery/Gur
Sugar (white)	Chinī
Sweets	Mitāi
Syrup	Chashnī/Sheera
Tea	Chai
Vinegar	Sirkā
Yeast	Khameer

12 The language barrier

Many Asians will probably never learn enough English to cope with all the situations they are likely to meet. There are various reasons: age, education, lack of opportunity, lack of confidence. Many have little contact with English-speakers, and what contact they have is rarely of a kind that will help them to learn the language.

With certain patients, therefore, health workers will always be operating across a language barrier and will require all their skills of tolerance and adaptability.

How much English does your patient know?

This can be very deceptive. People's English may be patchy. A patient who can answer familiar questions may not actually speak or understand much English.

Many people have a superficial fluency. They pick up phrases they hear frequently, such as greetings and simple questions about name and address. They may also understand certain much-used words—clinic, milk, doctor, hospital, operation—many of which have been adopted in their own languages. Do not, however, assume that because a patient can respond to a greeting and to certain words he can understand anything else you say.

Patients with more English may be able to talk easily on a subject they are familiar with but may not understand another subject at all, although to you both subjects seem equally familiar. A patient may, therefore, lose the meaning of a conversation quite suddenly. It is important to be alert to this and to keep checking as the conversation progresses that you have not 'lost' your patient. For example, a mother who can talk about feeding her baby may not be able to describe its illness.

Even Asians with excellent English may lose some of it under stress. We can all become 'lost for words'. This is even more likely when we are speaking a foreign language. Patients with very little English may lose it altogether under stress; those who are normally fluent may become incoherent, and may revert to the intonation of their first language, which you may feel sounds abrupt or over-excited.

Look out during conversation for any signs which indicate you are not getting through—a glazed look, a change of behaviour, embarrassment, a fixed smile or just a repeated 'yes'.

The two exercises which follow will illustrate some of the points to bear in mind. In the first exercise are seven examples of a health worker talking to a mother who understands only a little English. Can you identify what she does wrong? Check with the points listed on pages 150–154.

EXERCISE 1   SIMPLIFYING YOUR ENGLISH

A   Well I think she's got a slight rash there, but nothing to be alarmed about. I shouldn't fret if I were you, it's just one of those things. Children often get a sort of goose pimply rash like that. It may be something she's eaten.
(see 4, 5 and 10)

B   Do you think you could just pop into the kitchen and get me a nice big bowl of hot water? Not boiling—just hot. Oh, and before you go, get me a clean towel could you?
(see 6 and 9)

C   She'll probably have to have a couple of stitches—stitches? Oh you know—like when you cut something, when you're making a dress for example and you take a pair of scissors, and you cut into the material, chop it out and then you get a needle and cotton and you stitch it all up. Stitch. Stitches.
(see 12 and 13)

D   This is going to be a little bit uncomfortable but it won't last long. It might sting a bit. Try not to tense up. Just relax.
(see 4)

E   You go clinic Monday. You bring baby, me weigh baby. Doctor see baby. Make baby well.
(see 8)

F   Your baby will be weighed and examined by one of the clinic staff and you will be told whether you have to see the doctor.
(see 4 and 7)

G   Sterilise the bottle every time you use it and never put a pillow in baby's cot.
(see 11)

POINTS TO CHECK

These should, of course, all be used judiciously. A fluent English speaker would be insulted if addressed in slow and simple sentences. Be aware of what each patient knows, doesn't know, or has learnt, and adapt your language accordingly. The first three points, and the last three (13, 14 and 15), apply to all your conversations.

1 *Speak clearly but do not raise your voice.* Talking loudly to a non-English speaker as if he were deaf is a natural reaction but it is very disconcerting for the listener.

2 *Speak slowly throughout.* Try not to speed up as you get more interested or more involved in your subject.

3 *Repeat when you have not been understood.* If you have said something as simply as possible and it has not been under-stood—try repeating the *same* sentence again. Don't change the words. If you do, you are giving the patient a whole new task. If you repeat the words you used the first time, they may begin to make sense.

4 *Use words the patient is likely to know.* If there are several words which mean the same, use the simplest and most common: 'start' and 'end', not 'commence' and 'terminate'. Try to avoid using words that are, for example, used only in connection with health. It is all too easy to slip into jargon or complicated language without being aware of it.
(see A, D and F)

5 *Be careful of idioms.* The meaning may not be at all clear to your patient: don't say 'fed up', 'start from scratch', 'spend a penny', 'red tape'.
(see A)

6   *Simplify the form of each sentence.* Every language has different ways of saying more or less the same thing. For example, there are many ways of asking somebody to get (fetch, bring, find) some water.

> Can you get me some water please?
> Would you mind getting some water?
> Could you possibly get me some water?
> Would you mind me asking you to get me some water?
> Have you got some water I could use?
> I'd like some water please.
> I think I'll need some water.
> Could I have some water please?
> Get me some water please.
> I shall need some water.
> Will you get me some water please?
> Pop out and get me some water, could you?

For somebody who is learning a foreign language, these different forms are unnecessarily complicated and difficult. Become aware of how varied and complicated 'ordinary' English can seem to a foreigner. Choose simple forms and use them consistently. This is easier to understand and will provide the patient with a good clear model to copy.
(see B)

7   *Use the simple forms of verbs: active, not passive.*

'The doctor will give you a blood test', *not* 'you will be given a blood test by the doctor'.
(see F)

8   *Don't speak pidgin English.* It does not help people to learn to speak English properly, it is not easier to understand and it can sound condescending.

'You should go to the clinic on Monday' is no more difficult to understand than 'you go clinic Monday'.
(see E)

9   *Give instructions in a clear, logical sequence.* Even if the patient does not understand the words 'first' and 'then', she is likely to do things in the correct order because that is the order in which she heard them.

Say 'First sterilise the bottle. Then rinse it.'

Do not say, 'Rinse the bottle after you sterilise it'

or 'Don't rinse the bottle until you have sterilised it'

or 'Before you rinse the bottle, sterilise it'.

The words, 'before', 'after', 'until', which indicate the order to doing things, are fairly complicated and are often misunderstood.
(see B)

10 *Simplify the total structure of what you want to say in your mind before you begin.* If you are giving instructions or explaining something, break your topic down into clear, logical stages before you start. Don't try to simplify it as you go along, but look at what you want to explain and work it out clearly and simply in your own mind before you begin.

Simplifying is not the same as condensing. If you condense what you say, you make it *more dense* and often more difficult to understand. You avoid the natural repetition which we all use to help us follow a conversation. *A longer simplified explanation is easier to follow than a condensed one.*
(see A)

11 *Stick to one topic at a time.* Pause between topics, check
    that you have been understood, and signal clearly that you
    are moving on to a new topic.

    'Now I want to ask you about . . .'

    If you keep consistently to this form your patient will soon
    understand what you are doing.
    (see G)

12 *Be careful when you use examples.* People may become
    confused between your example, which you think is helpful,
    and what you are actually trying to convey.
    (see C)

13 *Use pictures or clear mime to help to get the meaning across.*
    When you find there are words that you often have difficulty
    with, cut out or draw some clear explanatory pictures and
    stick them on cards. Bring them out whenever you need
    them. For example, a cardboard clock face with moving
    hands can show time; simple and clear pictures of male and
    female bodies can be used for showing 'where it hurts'.
    Many excellent pictures and models can be found in toy
    shops. Note that photographs or realistic drawings are easier
    to understand than signs and symbols. Having a picture to
    look at or something to handle may also help to ease the
    tension of a difficult conversation.
    (see C)

14 *Judge how much people are likely to remember.* The effort
    of concentrating in order to understand can affect the
    memory very badly. Even people with no language problem
    only remember one or two points from each session. It may
    be useful to leave a simple note for the patient to read after
    you have left.

15 *Be aware of your language all the time.* Listen to yourself speaking and judge whether what you are saying is as clear as you can make it.

Making sure you have been understood

Develop a regular pattern of checking back. Do not move on to another point until you have checked that the earlier point has got through. There are various simple methods of checking back.

Try not to ask 'Do you understand?' or 'Is that all right?' You are almost bound to get 'yes' for an answer. 'Yes' is often the first word one learns in a foreign language. Saying 'yes' gets people off the hook. It does not necessarily indicate that they understand.

Try also to avoid questions to which a correct answer is 'Yes'. Phrase the question differently.

If you phrase the question so that the correct or required answer is 'No', there is a good chance that the person who answers 'No' has understood the question.

Ask the patient to explain to you what she is going to do. If the instructions are complicated, ask several simple questions rather than one long one. Don't accept a (possibly uncomprehending) repetition of what you have just said.

The second exercise gives eight extracts from conversations between a health worker and a mother with a young baby. In which of these has the health worker checked that the mother understands?

EXERCISE 2 CHECKING BACK

1 Health worker   Do you drink a lot of milk?
  Patient   Milk, yes.
  Health worker   Good.

2 Health worker   Is baby eating any solids yet?
  Patient   Yes.
  Health worker   That's nice.

3 Health worker   Take one of these pills after breakfast and one before you go to bed. Do you understand?
  Patient   Yes.

4 Health worker   Get baby weighed first and then go to see the doctor. Then come to see me. Now what are you going to do?
  Patient   Baby weighed.
  Health worker   Yes, and then what?
  Patient   Go and see doctor.
  Health worker   And then what?
  Patient   See you.

5 Health worker   Is baby still vomiting?
  Patient   No.
  Health worker   Has he been sick again?
  Patient   No.

6 Health worker   Does baby have tins? Baby tins?
  Patient   Baby tins.
  Health worker   Well I think that should be all right for him at the moment.

7 Health worker   You're giving him oranges are you? Good. Plenty of fruit juice? Fruit juice? Good. And he's getting his milk OK? Milk OK?

	Patient	Yes.
	Health worker	Good. Well he's a fine little boy isn't he?
	Patient	Yes.
8	Health worker	Are you taking any pain killers—aspirin, Panadol, Hedex or something?
	Patient	Aspirin.
	Health worker	Well that should take the pain away.

1 Not checked—mother may be merely repeating the word 'milk'.

2 Not checked—'yes' doesn't necessarily indicate a positive reply.

3 Not checked.

4 Checked—mother is asked to repeat the instruction.

5 Checked—the answer 'no' to both questions indicates that the mother has understood.

6 Not checked—'baby tins' may be just repetition.

7 Not checked.

8 Not checked—'Aspirin' may be the only one the mother has heard of, or may be just repetition.

Language and behaviour

Have you ever been in a foreign country where you could not speak the language? If you cannot understand what is being said, particularly by those in authority, and you cannot express yourself or answer questions, you may behave quite differently from the way you behave using your own language.

You may feel that everybody is talking about you. You may become extremely sensitive to their unconscious, non-verbal signals: body language, tone of voice, eye contact, impatient gestures.

You may become very tired, even during a short conversation.

You may avoid contact with people you cannot understand because you do not want to feel stupid and humiliated.

You may go ahead and do things you are not sure about without checking or asking advice.

You may remain passive and silent rather than initiate conversation, in case you get out of your depth.

You may settle for a simple, though inaccurate, explanation, and give up the attempt to express the complete truth which requires more complicated language.

You may pretend you understand to avoid exasperating the questioner and forcing him to repeat the whole thing all over again.

You yourself may have noticed in your work that, when you are talking to people who are difficult to understand, you sometimes switch off and give up the struggle to understand what they are trying to say.

157

Making sure you understand

It is important to remember how nervous some people may be if they are ill or worried and know that they cannot explain properly. The behaviour you then see does not necessarily reflect the personality of your patient. Be aware, therefore, of any judgments you are making about the behaviour or personality of someone whose mother tongue is not English.

We interpret feelings through language: through what people say, how they say it and how they sound. In a second language a person often cannot choose the impression he gives; he has to say what he can as best he can, unaware of how it sounds to English ears. We all have a strong instinctive reaction to something that to us sounds rude, aggressive, demanding, or off-hand. We react to the words, tone of voice, pronunciation, stress and the use of or lack of polite forms. But we cannot apply these judgments reliably to someone whose mother tongue is not English. First, he does not have the full language to choose from. Second, he may not be aware of the implications we attach to his tone of voice, and so on. Many of the intonations and stress patterns of Northern Indian languages, for example, sound abrupt or rude to English ears.

The stress and intonation of a foreign language are also the most difficult things for an adult to learn. Even people who speak apparently fluent English are usually still affected by the patterns of their mother tongue.

Correct polite forms are also very much a question of language and culture. For example, there are no words for 'please' and 'thank you' in many Asian languages. Politeness is indicated by the choice of verb and in other ways. Phrases such as 'I want' 'you must' are perfectly polite in Asian languages because there are several choices of verb forms, and of pronouns (like 'vous' in French and 'Sie' in German), which indicate politeness.

If somebody sounds rude or off-hand, stop and consider whether it is likely that he would wish to be so. It is far more likely that he is saying the only words he knows, or that he is trying to transfer the words, forms and intonations of his own language directly to English. A person who is dependent on you is unlikely to wish to antagonise you. You are usually the one in control, you have initiated the conversation and you wish to have a positive working relationship. So the onus is on you to exercise considered tolerance and understanding of your patient's difficulties with English.

13 Asian languages

There are four main facts about language which you should know for each patient. It is useful to make a note about them in the patient's record.

1 The first language (mother tongue) of the patient.

2 Any other language the patient speaks or understands, and how well he or she speaks or understands them.

3 What language(s), if any, the patient can read.

4 The relationship between the patient's own first language to other Asian languages. If you need an interpreter, and one speaking the patient's language is not available, you will have some idea of who else might be suitable. (See Figure 11, page 163.)

How many languages do most people speak?

There is no 'Indian language', any more than there is a 'European language'. People from different parts of the subcontinent speak different *languages,* not, as so many non-Asians seem to believe, different dialects. (See Figure 1, page 6, and Maps 1 and 2, pages 8 and 9.)

161

Most Asians in Britain speak one of six languages: Hindi, Urdu, Punjabi, Gujarati, Bengali, Pashto. They may speak one of the dialects of the language: for example, Mirpuri, a dialect of Punjabi; Kutchi, a dialect of Gujarati. Which language or dialect they speak depends on where they come from. Some languages have some similarities, like Italian and Spanish; others are quite different, like Italian and Swedish.

People from East Africa speak the language of the area of the Indian subcontinent from which their families originated (mainly Gujarat and Punjab).

Many Asians speak more than one language. Sometimes the language they have used at school is different from their mother tongue, and so people who have spent several years at school speak both.

In the subcontinent, the official state language may be different again from an individual's mother tongue. The official language is used when people with different mother tongues need to communicate, or for official or business transactions, particularly in towns and cities. People who have had little education and who come from rural areas may speak only one language, their own mother tongue. But people who have a good deal of education, have lived in urban areas, or have been involved in business, speak several languages.

Are all their languages the same?

Most of the Asians in Britain come from the northern part of the subcontinent. Their languages belong to the Northern Indian group of languages. This is why some of the Asian languages we hear in Britain sound fairly similar.

The relationship between different Asian languages becomes very important when an interpreter is needed. Figure 11 shows these relationships.

Figure 11 RELATIONSHIPS BETWEEN ASIAN LANGUAGES

	HINDI	*URDU*	*PUNJABI*	*GUJARATI*	*BENGALI*	*KUTCHI*	*PASHTO*
HINDI		ALMOST EVERY-THING	QUITE A LOT	a little	nothing	a little	almost nothing
URDU	ALMOST EVERY-THING		QUITE A LOT	a little	nothing	a little	almost nothing
PUNJABI	QUITE A LOT	QUITE A LOT		a little	nothing	very little	nothing
GUJARATI	a little	a little	a little		nothing	QUITE A LOT	nothing
BENGALI	nothing	nothing	nothing	nothing		nothing	nothing
KUTCHI	a little	a little	very little	QUITE A LOT	nothing		nothing
PASHTO	nothing	nothing	nothing	nothing	nothing	nothing	

Note: The figure refers only to spoken languages, and shows roughly the extent to which one language is similar to or different from another. In their written forms, most languages are very different (see Figure 12, page 165).

Colloquial *Hindi* and colloquial *Urdu* are basically the same language, though there are some variations in pronunciation and vocabulary. Indians tend to use the name *Hindi*, and Pakistanis tend to use the name *Urdu*. It is important to note, however, that educated formal Hindi and Urdu, as taught in schools, differ a good deal. Educated formal Hindi uses a lot of Sanskrit words: educated formal Urdu uses a lot of Arabic words. People who only speak colloquial Hindi or Urdu cannot understand formal Hindi or Urdu. (The British in India used the term 'Hindustani' to describe colloquial Hindi or Urdu. The term is not used any more.)

Reading and writing

There are three alphabets: Devanagri, Gurmukhi and Arabic. The Roman alphabet of the European languages is not used.

IN INDIA

PUNJABI is written in the *Gurmukhi* alphabet.

GUJARATI is written in the *Devanagri* alphabet.

HINDI is written in the *Devanagri* alphabet.

IN PAKISTAN

URDU is written in the *Arabic* alphabet.

PUNJABI is written in the *Arabic* alphabet.

PASHTO is written in the *Arabic* alphabet.

IN BANGLADESH

BENGALI is written in the *Devanagri* alphabet but in a form very different from that used for Gujarati and Hindi.

Kutchi and Mirpuri are very rarely written because they are
dialects of Gujarati and Punjabi, respectively, and are not taught at
school. Urdu is the language of all schooling in Pakistan: most
Pakistanis who can read and write will therefore use Urdu.

Figure 12 shows how the same sentence will appear when written
in six different Asian languages and in the three different alphabets.

Figure 12 WRITTEN FORMS OF ASIAN LANGUAGES

English
Please give your name to the nurse before you sit down.

Bengali (Devanagri alphabet)

(Rough transcription: deya kariya nurs ke apana naam diya boshen.)

Punjabi (Gurmukhi alphabet)

(Rough transcription: kerpa karke bettan ton* pehla* nurs kohl apana na*
likhao.)

Hindi (Devanagri alphabet)

(Rough transcription: meherbani karke bettne se pehle nurs ke paas apana
naam likhvai*.)

continued over

Punjabi (Arabic alphabet)

مہربانی کرکے بیٹھن توں پہلاں نرس کول اپنا ناں لکھواؤ

(Rough transcription: kerpa karke bettan ton* pehla* nurs kohl apana na* likhao.)

Urdu (Arabic alphabet)

مہربانی کرکے بیٹھنے سے پہلے نرس کو اپنا نام بتلا دیں

(Rough transcription: meherbani karke bettne se pehle nurs ko apna naam batalade*.)

Gujarati (Devanagri alphabet)

મહેરબાની કરી બેસતાં પહેલા
નર્સ ને તમારું નામ લખાવો

(Rough transcription: merherbani kari ne besta* pahele nurs ne tamara naam lukhao.)

*Nasal vowel sound.

It should be remembered that, because in their written form the Asian languages use three different alphabets, someone who can *speak and understand* several Asian languages may only be able to *read and write* his own. It is important, therefore, to ensure that notices and leaflets are translated into all alphabets and languages used by the local Asians, using a *simple colloquial* style rather than a formal style.

Remember that older people, women and people from less developed areas may have had little or no formal education. They may not be able to read or write at all.

English in the Indian subcontinent and East Africa

English has widespread official use in India, Pakistan and Bangladesh, but it is only spoken and written by people with considerable education, and it is taught at school. English is more widely spoken in Southern India, where it takes the place of Hindi as the major national language. It is generally the first language of East African Asians from Goa. Many Asians in Britain, therefore, may be able to read and write some English even if they cannot understand or speak it.

Where English has been used by Asians as the language of administration and business, it has developed as a distinctive language of its own. We may call it 'Indian-English'. It is in many ways different from the English spoken in Britain (British-English), and has been much influenced by the first languages of the people who speak it. The grammar, inflexions and stress patterns of Northern Indian languages have become part of standard Indian-English.

Indian-English has become an acceptable language in its own right in India and East Africa. It has a distinctive sound and vocabulary. People who speak it understand each other perfectly, although people in Britain may not understand them half so well. Asians who have learned and used English successfully in Asia or East Africa may be very surprised to find that they do not always understand the English spoken here, and that British people may have problems understanding them.

As a summary, there follow examples of the language abilities of five Asian patients.

Joginder Singh Sidhu
from Punjab, India

mother tongue: Punjabi

at school: used Punjabi

reads and writes: : Punjabi (in Gurmukhi alphabet)

Mohammed Khaliq from Mirpur District, Pakistan	*mother tongue:* Mirpuri (a dialect of Punjabi)
	at school: used Urdu
	reads and writes: Urdu (in Arabic alphabet)
Fatma (wife of Mohammed Khaliq)	*mother tongue:* Mirpuri (a dialect of Punjabi)
	did not attend school: cannot read or write
Nareshlal Dasani from East Africa (family from Gujarat)	*mother tongue:* Gujarati
	at school: (in East Africa) used Gujarati; learned to speak and read and write Hindi, and to read and write English
	reads and writes: Gujarati and Hindi (in Devanagri alphabet); also reads and writes, but does not speak much, English
Mohammed Ali from Bangladesh	*mother tongue:* Bengali
	at school: Bengali
	reads and writes: Bengali (in Devanagri alphabet)

14 Interpreters

An interpreter will be needed for a medical conversation if a patient speaks little or no English, or if his language ability falls far below its normal level due to stress.

'Speaking' a language can mean anything from real fluency to some kind of pidgin communication. It is necessary to get this clear with your interpreter. If he says he can speak two languages, he may mean that he can get by in a second language because it is related to his first language (like an Italian who has never learned Spanish but who can communicate to some extent with Spanish-speakers because Italian and Spanish are somewhat similar.) On the other hand, he may mean that he has learned, and regularly used, the second language.

It is extremely important for a health worker who uses someone to interpret to be aware of exactly what is happening. Interpreting is a skill. It is no less a skill to know how to use an interpreter.

Many health workers do not have regular access to a trained interpreter. They may have to use a member of the patient's family, a neighbour, another patient, or another health worker. Non-professional interpreters are often well-meaning, but their efforts to help may be clumsy and inadequate, and sometimes confusing rather than clarifying, given the subtlety and sensitivity which may be needed. But, until all hospitals and health service agencies whose catchment areas contain Asian communities employ competent interpreters, we shall have to use whomever we can get.

The interpreter who can best serve your needs

is fluent in both English and the patient's language

has some training in interpreting

has some medical knowledge, and knowledge of how the health services work

accompanies you every time you visit the patient

is acceptable to, and trusted by, the patient

is sensitive to both your needs and those of the patient

takes a neutral role

puts the patient at ease

has a good memory and pays careful attention to detail

can translate fine shades of meaning

tells you when she has difficulty in translating what you have said, and explains why

is aware of cultural expectations or attitudes--yours and your patient's--and can explain things to both of you when needed

can tell you a good deal about the patient from her own observation after the interview

The health worker and the interpreter, therefore, are a working pair who each contribute to the other's understanding. The health worker remains in control of the progress and direction of the conversation, while the interpreter uses her own sensitivity and understanding to give additional insight into the patient's problems. Time, mutual trust and cooperation are required to achieve this kind of relationship.

Points to check when you are using an interpreter

1 Do the patient and the interpreter speak the same language?

In one important respect interpreting may be difficult, even if two languages are close. Most languages have colloquial terms for various parts of the body and for certain illnesses. A Hindi-speaking interpreter, for example, may not understand the colloquial terms used by a Punjabi-speaking patient, and the patient may not know any other way of describing her problem. Try, therefore, to get an interpreter who comes from the same area as the patient.

2 Have you checked the interpreter's ability?

You may be able to do this by getting someone else who speaks both languages to listen to the interpreter at work.

If it seems that the interpreter does not understand the patient or is not interpreting exactly, it is important to find out why. It may be necessary to find another interpreter.

3 *Are you controlling the conversation?*

Have you decided, and told the interpreter, whether you want word for word translation or whether you want her to translate fairly freely? How have you decided this?

4 *Is the patient embarrassed by the interpreter?*

A patient may accept a doctor or other health worker of the opposite sex because professional training and status are respected. But the interpreter must be of the same sex as the patient, and is more likely to be accepted if he or she is older and married.

5 *Does the patient trust the interpreter?*

The patient will not answer all the questions truthfully if she does not trust the interpreter completely. Be careful whom you use to interpret anything that the patient would not want widely known. Would you, for example, want to communicate intimate, personal details through the people next door?

6 *Is the patient prevented from telling you everything because of his/her relationship with the interpreter?*

Using a member of the family for anything beyond the translation of simple factual questions or instructions can be unreliable and upsetting. There are many things a mother will not wish to tell her child. If a child whose English is good is used to interpret frequently, normal family relationships can be badly disrupted. There are many topics for which children must never be used to interpret. Children may be kept off school to interpret for their parents. Teachers become angry about this and even more pressure is placed on the child.

A husband or wife may also be undesirable as an interpreter. Patients may not wish to tell their spouse everything that they wish to tell the health worker. There is also the danger that a family member will not translate directly but will be reticent about some things, add an explanation, or put his or her own interpretation on the facts.

7 *Is the interpreter translating exactly what the patient is saying or is she putting in her own views and interpretations?*

You may have an amateur diagnostician between you and your patient! The interpreter may be tempted to re-interpret what the patient says as well as to translate it. Her own attitudes may influence her translation. This is more likely when the interpreter is close to the patient.

The interpreter may identify either with you or with the patient. She may be blamed, by you or the patient, for what she translates, for not making things clearer, or for not being more helpful. She may sometimes be in the difficult position of knowing that the response of one of you is wrong, or that the advice she is being asked to translate is inappropriate. Being a meticulous and neutral mouthpiece is a very difficult job.

8 *Are you maintaining your relationship with the patient?*

Speak direct to the patient as much as possible. Look at the patient and not at the interpreter when you are speaking, even if the patient cannot understand you. Sit facing the patient. Express your feelings and sympathies towards the patient through the interpreter, just as you would if you and the patient could communicate directly. *When* the interpreter is interpreting, she is speaking for you or for your patient. *While* she is speaking, behave as you would if you yourself were speaking to the patient, or if she were speaking to you. Look at the patient, notice reactions, give reassuring nods and smiles, use the time to study your patient. If the patient speaks and understands even a little English, it may be possible for you to speak to her yourself most of the time and to bring in the interpreter only when you feel you are not getting through.

9 Are you offending the patient?

While the patient is in the room, do not discuss her, or anything you do not want her to know, with the interpreter. Most people understand more English than they speak; the patient may, therefore, understand a good deal of what you say to the interpreter and may become confused, anxious or offended.

10 Are you making things easy for the interpreter?

Speak clearly and slowly, use simple words and keep the style of what you say straightforward. Give the words in the way you would like them translated. If you don't, the interpreter will have to translate your message into simple English in her head first, before translating it into the patient's language.

Give simple but full explanations, just as you would to a British patient. But pause frequently to allow the interpreter to translate. Do not make too many demands on the interpreter's memory by giving long chunks of speech to translate.

11 Are you allowing enough time?

Interpreting is a slow business, much slower than ordinary conversation. Simultaneous interpreting is an extremely rare and difficult skill which many highly educated and articulate people take several years to master. Your interpreter needs time to listen to what is said, to assess it and to translate it.

Allow two or three times as long for a conversation when you are using an interpreter. Remember that language ability fails under stress; this is true for the interpreter as well as for the patient. Do not look at your watch or otherwise show impatience. Try not to interrupt while the patient and the interpreter are conversing. Do not cut down your explanation because you are short of time.

12 Does the interpreter understand the purpose of your questions?

A lot of what you say cannot be translated direct to make sense in Asian terms. The interpreter may be able to put things to the patient in a way that makes more sense than a direct translation of what you have said. She is more likely to be able to convey the meaning of your message if she knows exactly what your aims are.

13 Does the interpreter tell you when she is having difficulty, and why?

The patient may not understand certain medical or anatomical terms, and so may not understand certain questions even in her own language. The interpreter may have to give a lengthy explanation to the patient in order to get an answer to your question. She may find it very difficult to make the patient understand exactly what is being asked. It may also be difficult for the interpreter to translate to you what the patient is saying. The patient may have a strong regional accent, may be using colloquial terms the interpreter does not know, may speak too fast or meander because she is muddled or reluctant to answer. The interpreter must feel enough trust and confidence in you to tell you when things are getting difficult.

14 *Are you helping the interpreter to establish a good working relationship with the patient?*

Introduce the interpreter. Give her time to talk briefly to the patient and explain her background, before she starts interpreting. She may like to reassure the patient about her trustworthiness. She may wish to remind the patient to speak slowly and to allow time for the translation.

15 *Is the interpreter ashamed of the patient?*

The interpreter may come from a background very different from that of the patient. She may feel ashamed of the patient's behaviour, and embarrassed and defensive about Asian people and culture as a result. This can affect the translation you get.

An interpreter is also likely to react in this way if you show impatience, or if you treat her—because she, too, is Asian—as in some way responsible for how any individual patient behaves.

The interpreter may become defensive and embarrassed and may try to hide things about the patient or about Asian culture if she thinks you will disapprove, or she may distance herself from the patient and be chiefly concerned to show you that she shares nothing of the culture or attitudes of such people. In either case, communication between yourself and your patient is disastrously affected.

16 *Is the interpreter doing part of your job too?*

It is tempting when one is hard-pressed to delegate one's role when using an interpreter; for example, to leave her to give instructions or an explanation to a patient and to go off to see someone else. This puts pressure on the interpreter; she is being asked to do part of your job, and the patient will not trust her 'medical' authority.

Select bibliography

1 ANWAR, Muhammed. *Muslim burials: a policy paper.* London, Community Relations Commission, 1975. pp. 12.

2 BALLARDS, Roger *and* BALLARDS, Catherine. *The Sikhs: the development of south Asian settlements in Britain. in* WATSON, J.L., *editor. Between two cultures: migrants and minorities in Britain.* Oxford, Basil Blackwell, 1977. pp. 21–56.

3 BEAL, G.E. *Asian diet and health.* Southall (Middlesex), Community Education Team, 1976. pp. 19.

4 BENTHAM, I.A. *Tuberculosis: an old enemy stages a comeback. Nursing Mirror,* vol. 145, no. 23. 8 December, 1977. pp. 44–46.

5 BONAMY, David. *Immigrants from Bangladesh.* Southall (Middlesex), National Centre for Industrial Language Training (NCILT), 1978. pp. 100.

6 BRAH, Avtar. *South Asian teenagers in Southall: the perceptions of marriage, family and ethnic identity. New Community,* vol. VI, no. 3. Summer 1978.

7 CHEETHAM, J. *Social work with immigrants.* London, Routledge and Kegan Paul, 1972. pp. 240. *Library of social work.*

8 COMMUNITY RELATIONS COMMISSION. REFERENCE AND COMMUNITY SERVICES. *Refuge or home: a policy statement on the resettlement of refugees.* London, CRC, 1976. pp. 68.

9 COMMUNITY RELATIONS COMMISSION. REFERENCE AND TECH-
NICAL SERVICES DIVISION. *Aspects of mental health in a multi-
cultural society.* London, CRC, 1976. pp. 63.

10 COMMUNITY RELATIONS COMMISSION. REFERENCE AND TECH-
NICAL SERVICES DIVISION. *Who minds? A study of working mothers
and child minding in ethnic minority communities.* London, CRC, 1975.
vol. 1 (report) pp. 77, vol. 2 (summary).

11 COMMUNITY RELATIONS COMMISSION. SOCIAL SERVICES
SECTION. *A guide to Asian diets.* London, CRC, 1976. pp. 20.

12 CRISHNA, Seetha. *Girls of Asian origin in Britain.* London, YMCA of
Great Britain, 1975. pp. 45.

13 DAVITZ, L.L., *and others. Cross-cultural inferences of physical pain and
psychological distress—1,* by L.L. Davitz, J.R. Davitz *and* Y. Higuchi.
Nursing Times, vol. 73, no. 15. 14 April, 1977. pp. 521–523.

14 DAVITZ, L.L., *and others. Cross-cultural inferences of physical pain and
psychological distress—2,* by L.L. Davitz, J.R. Davitz *and* Y. Higuchi.
Nursing Times, vol. 73, no. 16. 21 April, 1977. pp. 556–558.

15 GHAI, D. *and* GHAI, Y., *editors. Portrait of a minority: Asians in East
Africa.* Second revised edition. Nairobi, Oxford University Press (East
Africa), 1972. pp. 238.

16 GREAT BRITAIN. DEPARTMENT OF HEALTH AND SOCIAL
SECURITY. Catering and Dietetic Branch. *Catering for minority groups.*
Health Service Catering Manual, vol. 6. (in press).

17 GREEN, W.J. *The health educator's responsibilities in a multi-cultural
society. Journal of the Institute of Health Education,* vol. 11, no. 1.
1973. pp. 7–12.

18 HIRO, D. *Black British, white British.* Harmondsworth, Penguin, 1973.
pp. 346.

19 HOLROYDE, Peggy, *editor. East comes west: background to some Asian
faiths.* London, Community Relations Commission, 1973. pp. 101.

20 HUNT, Sandra. *The food habits of Asian immigrants. in* VAN DEN
BERGHS AND JERGENS LIMITED. *Getting the most out of food.*
Burgess Hill, Van den Berghs and Jergens Limited, 1976. pp. 14–53.
Getting the most out of food (nutrition award) series number 11.

21 HUNT, Sandra. *Traditional Asian food customs. Journal of Human Nutrition,* vol. 31, no. 4. August, 1977. pp. 245–248.

22 JAMES, Allan G. *Sikh children in Britain.* London, Oxford University Press, 1974. pp. 124. *Institute of Race Relations Series.*

23 KHAN, Verity Saifullah. *Pakistani women in Britain. New Community,* vol. 5, nos. 1–2. Summer, 1976. pp. 99–108.

24 KHAN, Verity Saifullah. *The Pakistanis: Mirpuri villagers at home and in Bradford.* in WATSON, J.L., editor. *Between two cultures: migrants and minorities in Britain.* Oxford, Basil Blackwell, 1977. pp. 57–89.

25 KOHLER, David F., *editor. Ethnic minorities in Britain: statistical data.* Third edition. London, Community Relations Commission, 1974. pp. 20.

26 KUEPPER, W., *and others. Ugandan Asians in Great Britain,* by W. Kuepper, G. Lackey *and* E. Swineaton. London, Croom Helm, 1975. pp. 180.

27 MILNER, David. *Children and race.* Harmondsworth, Penguin, 1975. pp. 288.

28 PARRINDER, E.G. *Asian religions.* Second revised edition of *Introduction to Asian religions.* London, Sheldon Press, 1975. pp. 144.

29 POWER, Jonathan. *Western Europe's migrant workers.* London, Minority Rights Group, 1976. pp. 40.

30 ROSE, E.J.B. *Colour and citizenship: report on British race relations.* London, Oxford University Press, 1969. pp. 840. *Institute of Race Relations series.*

31 SHARMA, Ursula. *Rampal and his family.* London, Collins, 1971. pp. 222.

32 SMITH, David J. *The facts of racial disadvantage: a national survey.* London, PEP (Political and Economic Planning), 1976. pp. 307.

33 SMITH, David J. *Racial disadvantage in Britain: the PEP report.* Harmondsworth, Penguin, 1977. pp. 349.

34 STERN, V. *and* WALLIS, S. *Caring for under-fives in a multi-racial society.* London, Community Relations Commission, Reference and Technical Services, 1977. pp. 60.

35 STORER, J. *Hot and cold food beliefs in an Indian community and their significance. Journal of Human Nutrition,* vol. 31, no. 1. February, 1977. pp. 33–40.

36 TANDON, Yash. *Problems of a displaced minority: the new position of East African Asians.* Revised in 1978 by Arnold Raphael. London, Minority Rights Group, 1978. pp. 24.

37 TAYLOR, John H. *The halfway generation: study of Asian youth in Newcastle-upon-Tyne.* Windsor, N.F.E.R. Publishing Company Ltd., 1976. pp. 272.

38 WATSON, Peter. *editor. Psychology and race.* Harmondsworth, Penguin, 1973. pp. 491.

Index

INDEX

Modesty
  in daughters 18
  in washing, among women 105–6
  maintaining in hospital 115–16
Mohammed (prophet) 42 43 45
  Birthday of (Islamic festival) 48
Money
  attitudes to ownership 13
  sent home by emigrants 21 22
Moral code 18
  Islamic 44
Moral obligations of family members
    13–14
Moslems
  attitudes to arranged marriages 15
  attitudes to nurses 60
  behaviour of widows 16
  childbirth rites 75
  death and funeral rites 51–2
  naming system 94–8
    commonly used names 102
  prohibitions on women during
    menstruation 110
  religious jewellery 118
  restrictions on food 123–4
  showers preferred to baths 105
  women shave body hair after
    menstruation or childbirth 107
  women's clothes 113 114
  see also Islam
Mosques 45
  congregational prayer for men 43
  schools 45
Mourning 49
  Hindu signs of 51
Mouth, cleaning 108
Muharram (Islamic festival) 49

Names, transliteration into Roman
    alphabet 90
Naming systems 87–98
  Asian adapted to British usage 89 97
  British 88
  Gujarati Hindus 92
  Gujarati Moslems 98
  Hindu 90–2
    commonly used names 100
  Moslem 94–8
    commonly used names 102
    correct usage 97

Naming systems *(continued)*
  Moslem *(continued)*
    entering in British records
      95 96 97
    practical exercise 103–4
    role names 90
  Sikh 39 93–4
    commonly used names 101
Nanak, Guru 38
  Birthday of (Sikh festival) 42
Navratri (Hindu festival) 37
Necklaces, worn by Swami Narayan
    Hindus 117
Neem twigs 108
'Next-of-kin' alternatives 90
Non-violence, Hindu belief in 31
Nose
  cleaning 108
  jewels 118
Nurses 60
Nursing, by extended family 60
Nutanvash (Hindu festival) 37
Nutritional requirements and sources
    136–9

Oils
  rubbed into hair 107
  used after bathing 106
Old people 28–9
  changed role in Britain 29
  facilities at Sikh Gurdwaras 40
  supported by children 83
  to be shown respect by health
    workers 69
  western attitudes to 26
Outcastes 34
Ownership of money and property 13

Paneer 125
Patel 34
Patent medicines 62–3
Personal hygiene 105–11
  Islamic rules 47
  see also Washing rituals
Personal names 39
  in Hindu naming system 91
  in Moslem naming system 94–7
  in Sikh naming system 93
Physical handicaps 63–4
Pilgrimage to Mecca 44

186